D1553160

THE PARIS LECTURES

EDMUND HUSSERL

THE PARIS LECTURES

Translated by

PETER KOESTENBAUM

With an Introductory Essay

Second edition
Third impression

MARTINUS NIJHOFF

THE HAGUE

1975

FOR PHYLLIS

ISBN 90 247 5133 0

PRINTED IN THE NETHERLANDS

PREFACE

The present translation is based on the German original, which has been edited by Professor S. Strasser and published in *Husserliana–Edmund Husserl, Gesammelte Werke. Auf Grund des Nachlasses veröffentlicht vom Husserl-Archiv (Louvain) unter Leitung von H. L. Van Breda*, vol. I (The Hague: Martinus Nijhoff, 1950), pages 3–39.

Both my translation of the *Paris Lectures* and the *Introductory Essay* had been completed before the appearance of two substantial scholarly achievements: Dorion Cairns' faithful translation of Husserl's difficult *Cartesianische Meditationen* and Herbert Spiegelberg's detailed and comprehensive two-volume work, *The Phenomenological Movement*. I have since collated most carefully Professor Cairns' translation with my own in those passages which are similar in the German of the *Cartesianische Meditationen* and the *Pariser Vorträge*. As a result I was able to make several useful changes. Also, I have incorporated some material which had been unavailable to me prior to the publication of Professor Spiegelberg's work. However, I did not have the benefit of Dorion Cairns' *Guide for Reading Husserl*, which, at this writing, is not yet available in print.

I would like to express my gratitude to the publishers as well as to Dr. Herman Leo Van Breda, Rudolf Boehm, and to the Husserl Archives for their patience, encouragement, help, and suggestions.

San Jose, California.   P. K.
August, 1961

CONTENTS

INTRODUCTORY ESSAY

A. HUSSERL'S PHILOSOPHICAL POSITION

1. *Introduction*

The phenomenology of Edmund Husserl is perhaps the single most influential philosophic approach in the continent of Europe today, with significant ramifications in practically all intellectual and cognitive disciplines. The interest in phenomenology in the English-speaking world is growing at an accelerating pace.

The *Pariser Vorträge* (*Paris Lectures*) are a late, terse, sophisticated, and high-level summary of Husserl's philosophical position, and they may therefore serve as adequate introduction to his thought. The *raison d'être* of the present book is to help introduce the phenomenology of Edmund Husserl to English and American scholars. These lectures provide the foundation for what has been called Husserl's definitive work, the *Cartesianische Meditationen* (*Cartesian Meditations*), and trace in logical sequence the development of many doctrines central to Husserl's phenomenology. The lectures begin with deceptive simplicity, but increase quickly in difficulty and complexity. Difficult style, typical of Husserl, exists because of his proclivity for the pithy rather than the proverbial German love for the prolix. But his writings also are difficult because language and culture have failed to focus on those aspects of experience that he analyzes; he must consequently invent his language. Also, much obscurity exists because Husserl presupposes, in effect, familiarity with his views, language, and mode of expression.

The present essay is principally a brief and relatively simple exposition of Husserl's general philosophic position, with special reference to the *Pariser Vorträge*. Special effort is made in this essay to colligate continental philosophy with English and American trends.

A brief and general statement regarding Husserl's contribution to philosophy may be summarized in the following five points.

(1) Husserl's philosophical work takes its inception from mathematical and logical studies. He was interested in developing an analysis of the nature and warrant of mathematics and logic other than the then popular psychologism of John Stuart Mill, Theodor Lipps, and Herbert Spencer. Psychologism — a term used not only by Husserl, but also by other important students of mathematics and logic such as Bertrand Russell, Gottlob Frege, and Alexius Meinong — is the view that logical and mathematical laws are empirical generalizations about the thought-processes as these are determined by experimentation in psychology. Husserl sought a firmer foundation for logic, one that avoided the *reductio ad absurdum* of psychologism. His conclusions, however, differed substantially from those of modern mathematical logic.

(2) Husserl's researches in logic and mathematics led him to the thorough study of the precise appearance, manner of presentation, intuited structure, and the formation of logical "objects," as these objects manifest themselves when considered altogether removed from any adventitious psychological concomitants.

(3) Eventually Husserl generalized the methodology which he had developed for his logical analyses. The result was the method of phenomenology, which he felt was the *sine qua non* for genuine philosophical insights and progress. The outstanding features of phenomenology are these:

(a) Phenomenology is a method that presumes to be absolutely presuppositionless.

(b) Phenomenology analyzes data and does not speculate about world-hypotheses.

(c) Phenomenology is descriptive, and thus leads to specific and cumulative results, as is the case with scientific researches; phenomenology does not make inferences, nor does it lead to metaphysical theories.

(d) Phenomenology is an empiricism more adequate than that of Locke, more skeptical than that of Hume, and more radical than that of William James.

(e) Phenomenology leads to certainty, and is, consequently, an a priori discipline.

(f) Phenomenology is a scientific enterprise in the very best sense of that term, without at the same time being strictured by the presuppositions of science and suffering from its limitations. Furthermore, Husserl strongly believed that phenomenology can and does offer essential contributions to the foundations of science.

(4) In addition to providing insights about logic, the phenomenological technique as applied by Husserl resulted in the development of three major and important conclusions. The first of these was the "discovery" and the elaboration of the intentionality of experience. Husserl helped to disclose, in far more detail and with considerably more acuity and penetration than any previous thinker, the rich, varied, and complex nature of our contribution to experience. He developed multifarious careful analyses showing precisely how and to what extent the world is our construction. The second of these is the evocation and description of transcendental subjectivity, which is the unobserved observer that resides in all our perceptions, feelings, and thoughts. The explicit articulation of the idea of transcendental subjectivity is quite new to Western philosophy, whereas in the East it has been one of the oldest, most pervasive, and important insights. Finally, Husserl hints at a "transcendental idealism," which is perhaps his only quasi-metaphysical commitment — although he denies it. Many of his students and disciples, however, have abandoned him in these idealistic claims.

(5) The actual and potential influence of phenomenology is quite extraordinary. Phenomenology has rejuvenated many philosophical studies and given a particular fillip to realism in philosophy; it is also considered to be the methodological foundation and theoretical justification of existentialism. Phenomenology has lent itself particularly well to applications in psychology, psychiatry, and in the behavioral sciences generally. Furthermore, phenomenology has found its way into logic and mathematics, literary criticism, law and jurisprudence, and other disciplines.

2. *Premises*

To make Husserl's view intelligible, one must grant a number of important but suppressed premises. Attacks, actual and possible ones, from non-phenomenological sources are usually directed at these suppressed premises. No serious attempt is made here to defend these premises, but pointing out their existence facilitates the elucidation of Husserl's doctrines.

(a) The first premise must be that there are two current philosophical methodologies: philosophy is either the description and analysis of *language*, or, correlatively, that of *experience*. The possibility and justification of these methodologies are matters rarely studied in isolation. Much contemporary philosophy is being carried on without a clear understanding of this difference. In general, phenomenology — which is entrenched at present in the continent of Europe and from which ensued the burgeoning of existentialism — pursues an experience-oriented methodology; whereas positivism, naturalism, and the philosophies of analysis — more typical of England and America — follow language-oriented methods. To understand Husserl one must first grant that this distinction is actual and legitimate.

(b) The second premise is consequent to the first. It establishes the logical and ontological primacy of experience over language. The phenomenological method is the descriptive analysis of experience. The necessary presupposition, therefore, is that language embodies experiences, *i.e.*, that the structure of language is parallel to and representative of experience. The semantic or language-oriented approach assumes the converse to be true: language is logically, ontologically, and genetically prior to experience, and modifies and distorts experience. For the language-oriented method, the function of philosophy is to show the relation between philosophic problems — or "puzzles," as these are often called — and both the grammar and function of language. The assumption inherent in the semantic approach is that at least some, and perhaps all, philosophical problems are the logical consequences of quasi-grammatical errors or of ambiguities in the use of language. Husserl must be understood to assume that language reflects the structure of experience, or, if it does not, that we can examine experience independently of language. It follows that the analysis of experiences, with all their subtleties, is the presuppositionless beginning of philosophy.

(c) There is no absolute criterion of precision. Precision is a function of context and subject-matter. Already Aristotle, in his *Nichomachean Ethics*, and Mill, in his *Utilitarianism*, refer to what might be called the "principle of contextual precision." To accept Husserl's analyses we must grant that *vague* experiences are legitimate objects of philosophic scrutiny. We cannot restrict our efforts to the simple, the clear, and the distinct. For example, the structures of experience that are analyzed under "ego," "intersubjectivity," "horizons," "transcendental subjectivity," "*Lebenswelt*," "intentionality," and the like, are neither clear, simple, nor distinct. Quite to the contrary, the *analysandum* consists of obscure, fuzzy, and cloudy clusters of experience. Therefore, the present premise is that precision, *i.e.*, clarity and distinctness, is a variable, one that is a function of context. The same premise is prerequisite to accepting, even in principle, the existentialist analyses of guilt, anxiety, death, my body, encounter, freedom, boredom, *Mitsein*, self-deception, and transcendence.

(d) The fact that the experiences analyzed are often vague does not diminish their *certainty*. We can deny neither the existence nor the importance of these experiences. The world in which I live, my *Lebenswelt*, may contain extremely vague clusters of experiences; yet these experiences exist, are important, and lend themselves to descriptions with ever-increasing precision, accuracy, and reliability. The meaning and value of literature, poetry, and the other arts are predicated on the same assumption. Art explores experiences that are as vague as they are certain and important. Metaphors and numerous other devices are thus needed to effect communication and expression in art. The fourth premise, therefore, is that certain vague experiences must and can be analyzed because they are both certain and important. The tendency in non-phenomenological approaches has been to ignore any experience that cannot be placed into sharp focus by terming these meaningless, or relegating these to the status of "mere" emotive ejaculations.

(e) Since philosophy begins *in medias res*, it is sound in logic and necessary in practice to analyze some terms and their corresponding experiences without prior definitions. This point was made explicit by Whitehead, when he wrote,

> ...of course you have got to start somewhere for the purposes of discourse. But the philosopher, as he argues from his premises, has already marked down every word and phrase in them as topics for enquiry.[1]

For example, it must be seen as legitimate to analyze the ego without first defining the term. We assume that the word "ego" has some sort of "natural" referent — perhaps derived from ordinary use and quotidian experience — whose structure we can analyze and describe without further need for definition. Just as a landscape can be "described" — *i.e.*, reproduced — without more than cursory "framing," so the experience of the ego can be examined, reproduced, and described without further definition. The quest for precision through successive definitions leads to an infinite regress reminiscent of those of causation and deduction. These latter are meaningless if we deny them a first term. Similarly, the meaning of definition is reduced to absurdity when we press for an infinite regress. This "paradox of definition" must be invoked in Husserl's discussion of the ego, the "I," consciousness, world, other minds, etc. Regardless of the complexities of the problem suggested here, its satisfactory solution must be assumed in order to make sense of Husserl's view — as well as of almost any other philosophical position.

(f) Husserl frequently uses the term "transcendental." The penultimate premise, therefore, is that transcendental terms are non-contradictory and thus meaningful. The notion of transcendental terms springs from scholastic philosophy, and later assumed particular importance in the philosophy of Kant. In general, a term is used in a transcendental sense if it applies or refers to all of experienced being. If we make the additional distinction between "experienced being" and "unexperienced being" (*i.e.*, Kant's phenomena and noumena respectively), then the term "transcendent" refers to characteristics of unexperienced being, whereas the term "transcendental" designates properties pervasive in experienced being alone. However, in Husserl's later, idealistically oriented writings, this ontological bifurcation of being is questioned, and even rejected. In that case, a transcendental term designates a ubiquitous property of being *per se*, unqualified and absolute.

[1] A. N. Whitehead, *Modes of Thought*, lecture 9, N.Y.: The Macmillan Co.

That is to say, if x is a transcendental term which refers equally to any and all events, qualities, and relations (such as the characteristic of "possessing some form of being"), then x has what may be called ubiquitous reference, and the term is useless, meaningless, and, of course, indefinable. Unless we grant, as premise, the legitimacy of using terms in a transcendental sense, such statements as "All being is phenomenal," "All being is experienced by the ego," "All being is constituted in consciousness," "Transcendental subjectivity is at the core of all presentations" — all of which are essential to an understanding of Husserl's phenomenology — are meaningless.

"Being" is the transcendental term par excellence. Such terms, however, are subject to a number of logical difficulties. If a term has meaning through delimitation, "de-finition," that is, through negation, then transcendental terms have no meaning. They deny or negate nothing because they refer to everything. Also, all transcendental terms must have the same meaning — which in fact they do not — since they possess identical, that is, total, extension. This fact holds if we include in the terms extension properties as well as substances. Also, transcendental terms cannot be defined either *per genus et differentiam specificam* or ostensively. Since Husserl deals with the ubiquitous traits of being, with the categories present in experience, he must assume that the analysis of transcendental traits is possible without contradiction or other inherent difficulties.

(g) At the risk of paradox, one more assumption must be listed. The general purpose, which is one that can be realized, of philosophy is to seek for the *absolutely presuppositionless*. The exploration of the presuppositionless is essential for the foundation of any cognitive discipline whatever, and is the only path to certainty. In fact, "to be presuppositionless" and "to be certain" are synonymous expressions. Consequently, towards the end of his life, Husserl could ironically and yet proudly refer to himself as a person who in his old age "reached the perfect certainty that he can call himself a *true* beginner." [1]

---

[1] Herbert Spiegelberg, *The Phenomenological Movement* (The Hague: Martinus Nijhoff, 1960), pp. 153–154; quoted from the English preface to Husserl's *Ideen*.

3. Husserl's Program

Husserl's program in the *Pariser Vorträge*, as suggested by the title of his ensuing *Cartesianische Meditationen*, is significantly and deliberately similar to Descartes' work of that name. Eliciting the parallelisms between these two works will help us understand the underlying goals of Husserl's lectures, and, consequently, of his life's work.

(a) There is a fundamental kinship between Descartes' method of universal or systematic doubt and Husserl's phenomenological technique. Husserl acknowledges his debt to Descartes, and uses it to gain the ear of his French audience. The nature of Descartes' method can be seen when the French philosopher writes, in his "First Meditation," about "the general overthrow of all [his] former opinions." Descartes continues, "I shall be justified in setting all of [my former opinions] aside, if in each case I can find any ground whatsoever for regarding them as dubitable." In his "Second Meditation" he writes, "I shall proceed by setting aside all that admits even of the very slightest doubt, just as if I had convicted it of being absolutely false." Husserl's phenomenological epoche, on the other hand, his notion of bracketing or *Einklammerung*, consists in adopting a reflective and disengaged attitude towards our experiences. Only through his epoche can experiences be properly described and analyzed. Descartes discards all his beliefs; Husserl, through the epoche, performs an operation which has a similar effect; he suspends judgment. Husserl brackets specifically the existence and reality of an external world — the beliefs pervading all experiences. In this way Husserl manages to focus solely on the presentational structure of phenomena, that is, on phenomena as these appear prior to any interpretations or beliefs attached to them. The fundamental similarity of these methods is evident.

(b) Descartes' *indubitandum* — his *"cogito, ergo sum"* — has introduced into modern philosophy the dilemma of the egocentric predicament, the emphasis on subjectivity, the propensity for idealism, and the danger of solipsism. Specifically, however, Descartes' reversion to the *ego* in his epistemology and in his metaphysics has placed responsibility for ultimate normative and ontological decisions on the final source of subjectivity itself, not on some external criterion or authority. Husserl develops this theme at length through his concept of the transcendental Ego, his analysis of intentionality, and the general idealistic strain of his thought. The ontological significance of subjectivity has become a major concern for existentialist philosophy.

(c) Descartes worked for scientific reform in philosophy. Impressed with the advances and agreement in science and mathematics, he sought parallel rigor and success for philosophy. Husserl has similar intentions: he wishes to make philosophy into a science. He conceives it to be the function of philosophy to be a corpus of the most general empirical knowledge, where progress, unanimity, and cooperative research are possible.

(d) To Descartes, metaphysics was the foundation, the roots, in his tree of knowledge. Husserl, similarly, sees philosophy as the indispensable foundation for scientific advance: phenomenology must provide the theoretical foundations for modern science. Husserl's intent also bears significant resemblance to the contemporary philosophies of analysis. To the latter, philosophy's principal contribution is the clarification of the logic and language of science. For Husserl, philosophy as phenomenology examines those underlying constitutions and intentions of consciousness which make science possible in the first place.

Husserl's purpose and the significance of his approach can more clearly be brought into relief by noting the extent to which his views differ from those of Descartes.

(e) For Descartes, the ego, his *indubitandum*, serves as first axiom in a long deductive chain. Descartes' methodology and system are strictly patterned by him, in spirit at least, after the procedures of mathematics and logic. Husserl focuses his analysis on experience, not deduction. Husserl's early training and extensive work in the philosophy of mathematics apprised him of the difference between the deductive nature of mathematics and the impenetrable mysteries of irrational experience. He wishes to discover and describe the given in experience; he looks for the immediate data of consciousness, pure experience, presentation. Descartes' orientation is rationalistic, Husserl's is empirical. As a matter of fact, Husserl's position, even more than the pragmatism of William James, is, as stated before, a monumental attempt at radical empiricism.

(f) Descartes succumbs to what Gilbert Ryle terms the

"category mistake" by rendering the ego a *substantia cogitans*, a ghost in a machine. Husserl criticizes Descartes on the same grounds. The thoroughgoing empiricism of phenomenology purifies experience of assumptions, inferences, and unwarranted reifications; therefore, the ego is interpreted by Husserl as pure subjectivity as a central locus in all experience from which emanate all our conscious acts. "Pure subjectivity" may be a vague term, whereas "*substantia cogitans*" is, at least *prima facie*, a lucid metaphor. Analytical philosophy may be inclined to reject both terms: the former on the grounds that it is vague, and the latter on the grounds that it is meaningless. Husserl, however, rejects only the term "*substantia cogitans*"; and he does that because experience does not disclose such an event. He accepts the term "pure subjectivity" as a description of some of the actual and pervasive facts of human experience, vague as it may be, because that concept serves as index to an important locus in all experience, a locus of whose experienced existence we are certain.

(g) Descartes concludes his *Meditations* by establishing the independent existence of a second non-conscious, non-mental (in Kant's nomenclature, "transcendent" and "noumenal") substance, the *res extensa*. The proof for the existence of this material substance depends not only on the validity of his prior proof for the existence of God, but on the even more fundamental premise that the laws of causation and of deductive reasoning are binding on being itself. Descartes' position implies that these laws are not arbitrary or analytic, but coercive on the processes of the mind and the events in nature; these laws must apply not only to the phenomenal realm, but to the noumenal one as well. In other words, Descartes must assume that causation and deduction can legitimately be applied to inferences that lead our thought beyond all possible experience. Husserl's name for this Cartesian dualism — which has engendered the modern version of the epistemological problem of the existence of an external world and has had its logical outcome in Hume's skepticism — is "transcendental realism." Husserl rejects altogether this problematic Cartesian dualism. He prefers what, in effect, looks very much like a complex version of William James' neutral monism.

(h) Descartes' method of systematic doubt differs from the

phenomenological epoche in that the former makes no distinction whatsoever between the engaged or natural attitude (Dorion Cairns refers to it as experience or "objects *per se* or *simpliciter*") [1] and the disengaged, distanced, reflective, spectatorial attitude characteristic of the epoche.

(i) Descartes' formula describing the fundamental epistemological act is *"ego cogito."* Husserl transforms this dyadic interpretation of experience into the triadic *"ego cogito cogitatum."* This change corresponds more closely not only to experience but also to language, where such simple conscious acts as perceptions are articulated in the triadic form "I see a chair." This change calls attention to the important fact of intentionality, an aspect of experience ignored by Descartes.

4. *Key Concepts in Husserl's Phenomenology*

Husserl's philosophical position, with the exception of his logic, can be presented in terms of the key concepts developed in the *Pariser Vorträge*. The first of these is the phenomenological epoche (ἐποχή).

(*a*) *The Phenomenological Epoche.* Husserl's unqualified and radical empiricism is evident when he writes, "we must not make assertions about that which we do not ourselves *see*" (p. 9). If we use the terms "experience" and "scientific" with wide extension, we can say that the phenomenological method is scientific: in it, truth is determined exclusively by reference to the structure of experience in the precise and unadulterated form in which the latter presents itself to us. For confirmation we must always turn *zu den Sachen selbst*, to the things themselves, where *"Sachen"* or "things" refers not to physical objects but to any presentation or phenomenon whatever that may confront the ego in consciousness: *e.g.*, a chair, a star, a law of nature — such as that of universal gravitation —, a headache, the sense of impending doom, the law of contradiction, the square root of "−1," the idea of nothingness, etc.

In spirit, although not in results, the phenomenological method parallels the empiricism of the sciences. The difference rest

---

[1] Dorion Cairns, "An Approach to Phenomenology," in *Philosophical Essays in Memory of Edmund Husserl*, ed. Marvin Farber (Cambridge: Harvard University Press, 1940).

mainly on the facts that (i) phenomenology is science purified of unwarranted prior interpretations, constructions, and assumptions, and that (ii) phenomenology often is the description of the pervasive traits of experience, not the concern with regional specialties within experience, as is the case with laboratory sciences.

Descartes, concerned as he was with deductive proof, neglected this *description of experience*. British Empiricism is guilty of similar neglect. Its concern was with the question of cognitive import and warrant of sensory experience, not with the necessarily prior analysis of the nature of experience and the description of its structure. Yet Husserl has shown that descriptive research can modify, and in fact has modified, theoretical views in epistemology and metaphysics. Husserl, through the phenomenological epoche, addresses himself to this task of description. Description is the prerequisite and matrix for all philosophic problems.

"Epoche" is the Greek word for "bracketing." The method of phenomenology consists in focusing on any part or all of my experience, and then observing, analyzing, abstracting, and describing that experience by removing myself from the immediate and lived engagement in it. I must observe the experience in question from a distance, that is, from a state of reflection which is not unlike the conception of aesthetic experience in the theories of Bullough, Ortega y Gasset, and Schopenhauer.

Bullough and Ortega y Gasset interpret the aesthetic experience as the interposition of psychical distance between the object and ourselves. The difference between their views lies primarily in the amount of distance conducive to optimum aesthetic appreciation. In the aesthetic experience all but the object itself is, in a sense, bracketed; the object is extracted from the stream of practical, involved, committed, and engaged concerns in order that it may be contemplated, described, and analyzed in isolation, as it is in itself. In other words, in these doctrines the aesthetic attitude or psychical distance is requisite for knowing and discovering the immediate data of consciousness, the irrevocable structure of experience, the fundamental epistemological facts. "To bracket" means to put certain beliefs out of action or consideration. We may "bracket" the practical or scientific implications of an object or experience; we thereby suspend any judgment and disregard our beliefs that concern the practical or scientific affairs of the event in question.

We may also bracket, that is, leave out of consideration, epistemological and metaphysical theories that interfere with the pure and unadulterated apprehension of an event or experience. Finally, we may leave out of consideration the belief that the object under investigation possesses objective and independent existence or reality. Similarly, Schopenhauer interprets the Platonic Idea as viewing things independently of the principle of sufficient reason, independently of external relations, uses, theories, and emotional or scientific attitudes. For Schopenhauer, the Platonic Idea is the general type that an individual or a particular represents. He who can see the type or Platonic Idea as it inheres in the particular is the artistic genius. He who can detach an object from all connections and thus see how it participates in the Platonic Idea possesses an aesthetic experience. Only through distancing, bracketing, and reflecting can we see an object as it is in itself (that is, as it appears in itself), can we divorce an object from the projections of practical reason and the interpretations of our synthesizing consciousness. Thus, the aesthetic doctrines of Bullough, Ortega y Gasset, and Schopenhauer serve to suggest and illustrate Husserl's phenomenological epoche.

The familiar difference between, on the one hand, watching and enjoying a movie and, on the other, later analyzing its aesthetic, technical, and sociological aspects and implications may serve to illustrate the distinction between a natural or straightforward experience and that same experience bracketed. When I watch and enjoy the film I am "one with it"; I am engaged and involved. When, later, I analyze it, I distance myself from the straightforward experience of the film; I observe the film independently of my emotional involvement and identification with it. Criticism depends on the successful exercise of this latter attitude. When I bracket the reality of the film's contents by detaching myself from it, I consider the film as a film and not as a real state of affairs in which I participate. While engaged, I think of the events in the film as real: I view these as happening to me or around me. When distanced, I see the film for what it really is: an illusion. Film criticism invariably involves bracketing.

Bracketing our natural involvement with the film is not only necessary for the critical appraisal of the film, but it also enables us to analyze something that is closer to us than the object of apprehension: our personal mode of perceiving and reacting to the film. We can focus on the act and mode of perceiving as well as on the film itself. The examination of the act of perceiving — as will be discussed later — discloses an intimate relation between the act (the *cogito*) and the object (the *cogitatum*). The act synthesizes the object. The object, in other words, is said to be an intention: the object is meant and intended by the act. The act of apprehension constructs, fashions, *constitutes* the object. The precise nature of this process — central to epistemology — is discussed in Husserl's theory of intentionality. Eventually, through what Husserl calls successive "reductions," the focus can retreat even further from the objects (*cogitata*), behind the acts (*cogitationes*), and rest on the ego itself (*ego*). When the ultimate locus of apprehension and subjectivity has been reached, we understand and experience the true source of knowledge and constitution: the transcendental Ego.

The act of bracketing is parallel to Descartes' systematic doubt. The phenomenological epoche seeks to isolate the indubitable givenness in experience, operating under the traditional assumption that such givenness is the ultimate foundation for knowledge. C. I. Lewis' well-known conception of the given as that part of our experience about which we cannot possibly be mistaken[1] is in substantial agreement with the spirit of Husserl's quest.

In general, we must bracket, disregard, or suspend judgment about all our beliefs. This act entails a general disregard of what ordinarily is called "knowledge." Specifically it means, for Husserl, to bracket belief in the reality and existence of the external world, including, of course, the reality and existence of other minds. It is particularly interesting and important to note that what the epoche discloses as the *epistemologically*

---

[1] *Cf.* Clarence Irving Lewis, *An Analysis of Knowledge and Valuation* (La Salle, Ill.: Open Court, 1946), p. 183.

given is unchanged, in its nature and presentation, from what appears in the engaged or natural attitude. As a matter of fact, the epoche discloses the natural attitude precisely as it is in itself. Traditional conceptions of the given — such as sense data, raw data, presentations, pure experience — are, on the contrary, highly sophisticated, post-analytical philosophical constructions and inferences. In a real sense, "pure presentations," "uninterpreted sense data," and the like, are not given in experience at all: they are interpretations and constructions derived from experience. And about these putative immediate data of consciousness we can be very much mistaken.

That the epoche is the ultimate and hence presuppositionless perspective is evident. We cannot step back further than we can step back; we cannot disengage ourselves more than we can disengage ourselves. These propositions are true analytically.

Husserl's great influence on existentialism is due to the latter's reliance on the phenomenological method, especially the epoche. It is important to note, however, that Husserl's conception of phenomenology differs markedly from most of those who claim to have adopted it. To the existentialists, phenomenology is the disciplined, rigorous, sensitive, and imaginative description and analysis of the data of experience, particularly as these stem from the human situation and man's being-in-the-world. Husserl's phenomenology is more than that. Not only is Husserl's orientation preeminently epistemological rather than axiological, but his technique is more carefully delineated than it is for the existentialists. The details will appear in the subsequent exposition.

However, to justify Husserl's position we must introduce additional distinctions. These are two senses of the presuppositionless. On the one hand, "presupposition" is equivalent to "premise." Given the structure of arguments, a first argument, *i.e.*, an argument without a premise, is a self-contradictory concept. An argument without at least one premise is no argument at all. From the linguistic-logical point of view, the ideal of the presuppositionless cannot be achieved and must, hence, not be interpreted literally. From the experiential point of view, to seek the presuppositionless is to inquire about the ultimate cognitive perspective and stance of consciousness. This perspective is a matter of experience and intuition, not logical proof. The quest for such ultimate perspective, by means of the distance of the epoche, is a recession into subjectivity. The goal is reached when consciousness focuses on pure subjectivity: the pure subject of all apprehension. This matter will be discussed in greater detail under the transcendental Ego. Husserl seeks to describe experience; he eschews all cognitive claims. If we do not suppose, we do not presuppose either.

One consequence of the emphasis on the presuppositionless, and consequently a primary reason for the importance of the phenomenological epoche, is that the latter presumes to be the definitive manner in which the purely *given* in experience is to be uncovered and isolated.

The nature of the given thus disclosed as well as of the examples used differ markedly from the traditional analyses of the given. C. I. Lewis, for instance, writes about the steps of Emerson Hall[1]; the existentialists — who use Husserl's phenomenological technique — write about the human body, viscosity, anxiety, and death. The examples are different, and so are the extrapolations, generalizations, and inferences derived from them. Traditional empiricism concentrates on and finds the given in particular items of experience; phenomenology — when it is imbued with the spirit of ontology — describes the ubiquitous traits of experience; it seeks abstractions from experience and makes generalizations that are broader, but parallel in spirit, than those in science.

The epoche changes nothing in the world; however, the problem of the existence of the external world is bracketed and never reappears; it is never reintroduced. This problem, as also linguistic analysis has discovered, is dispensable.

But phenomenology also explores the specific structure, nature, and configuration of the individual data of experience. These data can be used for theory construction, for the confirmation of hypotheses, for mathematical insights, for intuitions into the experiences of being human, and the like. The data are called *cogitata* or objects. The data for examination need not be only sensory; they can also be eidetic or affective. That is to say, a concept — to the extent that it is apprehended by the ego, to the degree that it is a presentation to the ego — is an "object,"

[1] *Ibid.*, pp. 172 ff.

as Husserl uses that term. In the same way, an emotion — my own, first-person apprehension of that emotion — is an object, to Husserl's phenomenology. Questions of causal connections, origins, and statistical correlations are of only secondary importance. Phenomenology as conceived and developed by Husserl is indeed a first-stage scientific approach. That is to say, the first task of any scientific undertaking is the clear exposition of the data on which the discipline is grounded. The clarification of data is the first stage in the inductive sciences, as well as in deductive ones, and also in the linguistic clarification typical of modern philosophy. If there is any theoretical conflict between phenomenology and the experimental sciences, it is not to be found in the inductive techniques — phenomenology does not use inductive techniques, but it is not inimical to them either —, but in the definition of data. In the experimental sciences, as well as in common forms of empiricism and positivism, data are limited and highly interpreted and selected aspects of givenness. For phenomenology, on the other hand, anything whatever can serve as datum or as the epistemologically given. Every being, every aspect of experience, every event, all things are *given* in experience. The phenomenological epoche focuses on these. "Data," therefore, has a far wider extension for the phenomenologist than it does for the scientist. The restriction that science imposes on the concept of data has not been sufficiently analyzed philosophically. For example, why it is that one item of experience is properly a datum, whereas another item is not, is a matter that has not been given the attention by the scientific disciplines that it deserves. Once the proper attention is directed towards these problems, it will become immediately apparent that *any experience whatever, in the widest possible signification of that expression*, can serve — and must serve — as foundation-datum for our understanding of the world. To select certain experiences as bona fide data and concurrently reject others entangles us in important and unanalyzed epistemological and metaphysical commitments.

The relation between the phenomenological epoche and the epistemological problem of the given is explored in the first volume of Husserl's *Ideen zu einer reinen Phänomenologie und phänomenologischen Philosophie* (*Ideas*). Husserl accepts the general empiricist and positivistic position that sense data, or some reasonable simulacrum, are the genuine given. However, and importantly, Husserl expands, through the epoche, the notion of data to include universal concepts or essences. A logical or mathematical essence has a form of givenness that possesses important similarities to sensory forms of givenness. A logician using the epoche examines a logical essence just as a biologist examines a unicellular organism under a microscope. Both the organism and the essence are data given objectively, that is, in opposition and confrontation to the ego. The existentialists have expanded the notion of givenness even further by focusing the epoche on moods and other aspects of the human situation.

The given is a vast and much-explored topic in epistemology. Even in Husserl's analysis, many questions remain unanswered. Among these, two in particular emerge. First, in a sense everything is given. Even if we use the criterion that the given is that about which one cannot be mistaken and that which, in experience, is refractory and not of our own choosing, nonetheless, these properties have universal extension. Everything, *qua* presentation, even the most contrived, phantasmagoric, and erroneous construction, has its moments and aspects of untrammelled givenness in the above senses. If the presentations in question did not possess these moments of pure givenness, then they could not be subject to examination. It is an analytic truth that for a thing to be examined it must first be given. The epoche, thus, does not seem to isolate one area of experience alone and designate that area, and no others, as data.

Second, to the given is ascribed ontological priority. What are the grounds for such ascription? It seems that it is necessary to establish a commitment about what makes for proper interpretations and accounts of reality before an analysis of the given has any significance in the first place. The given is thus not the presuppositionless at all.

(*b*) *Intentionality and Constitution.* The application of the phenomenological epoche leads to the discovery that one of the most significant traits of experience is intentionality. This section deals with the general nature of intentionality, which includes some of the evidence adduced for the presence of intentionality, and it concludes with several miscellaneous aspects and problems arising within intentionality.

(i) The Nature of Intentionality. Husserl, following Brentano, holds that the essence of consciousness is intentionality. By this proposition he means that the object of my consciousness — a tree, an amoeba under a microscope, an electromagnetic wave, the logic of induction, a pain in my stomach, a complex number, Aquinas' conception of a First Mover, even my own subjectivity — is something meant, constructed, projected, constituted, in short, *intended* by me. Objectivity is a function and project of the subject. Consciousness is a stream between two poles: subject and object. Consciousness is a *vector* that effects an *organizational synthesis*. The intentional character of consciousness is carefully developed in his *Logische Untersuchungen* (*Logical Investigations*).

Intentionality is a discovery about the nature of consciousness. To the question "What is consciousness?" phenomenology answers "intentionality." Intentionality signifies the fact that consciousness is directional, that it is given in experience as an outward-moving vector. The source of the movement, the here-zone, is termed the ego, whereas the focus towards which the movement addressed itself, the there-zone, is the object. The division of the vector into ego, movement, and object is purely an abstraction, because another fundamental meaning of intentionality is the essential *unity of consciousness*. To be is to be the object to a subject *and* the subject for an object *at the same time*. An object (or objectivity) has meaning only to the extent that it is a given to a subject or an ego. Phenomenology protects itself from narrow idealism by also calling attention to the converse relation that defines consciousness: There is no meaning to the pure subject or isolated ego. A subject is what it is because objects are presented to it. To be a subject means to confront an object, just as to be an object means to be perceived by a subject. The essential inter-relationship and interdependency of subject and object is another central fact of experience designated by the term intentionality. Consciousness is a matrix for events; consciousness is the pre-condition for meaningful being; consciousness is subject-object encounter. Consciousness is not restricted to subjectivity — as

Cartesianism would have it — but arises through subject-object interaction.

The doctrine of intentionality is Husserl's highly sophisticated and richly developed version of the common epistemological position illustrated in the bifurcation that goes variously under the names of "knowledge by acquaintance" and "knowledge about," "pure data" and "inferences," "presentations" and "constructions," "the given" and "the interpreted," etc. Philosophers (and psychologists) have frequently held that the human mind makes substantial contributions to the specific structure of what appears before it, so that experience is construed to be a complex of data given externally and organizational principles supplied internally. The degree of organization from within the subject is a matter of dispute, but not the fact that such organization takes place. One of the most famous examples of this position is Kant's view that space and time are the pure forms of intuition: they are our subjective contributions to all sensory experience. We also see an illustration of the mind's contribution to the structure of the world in Kant's doctrine of the categories. The structure of the phenomenal realm, according to Kant, is a merger of, on the one hand, the pure qualia of giveness, which have a source external to the human mind, and, on the other, the pure forms of intuition and the categories. These latter are our own contribution to the nature and configuration of our conceptualized experience. Also, as is well known, the idealistic tradition which emanated from Kant, including Fichte, Schelling, Schlegel, Schopenhauer, and Hegel, holds that the world of our experience is partially created and structured by the perceiving ego.

Similarly, Josiah Royce held that the world is partly our own construction. He writes that we, as part of an eternal order, may well help *"to choose out and out* what world this fatal temporal world shall eternally be and have been. . . . This . . . was Kant's famous doctrine." [1] Roy Wood Sellars writes "the physical existent is not an object in its own right. It is *made* an object by the selective activity of the percipient organism." [2] Whitehead

[1] Josiah Royce, *The Spirit of Modern Philosophy* (Boston: Houghton, Mifflin & Co. Inc., 1892), p. 433.

[2] Roy W. Sellars, *Evolutionary Naturalism* (Chicago: Open Court, 1922), p. 44.

uses the term "decision" — meaning both cutting off and free choice — to designate an object of human experience.[1] Bergson subscribes to the epistemological view that cognition of the world involves subjective projection and organization. He maintains that "the intellect is characterized by the unlimited power of decomposing according to any law and of recomposing into any system."[2] He later asserts that

> the division of unorganized matter into separate bodies is relative to our senses and to our intellect .... Matter, looked at as an undivided whole, must be a flux rather than a thing.[3]

Bergson further writes that "in the continuity of sensible qualities we mark off the boundaries of bodies."[4] Finally, Blanshard, in his comprehensive *The Nature of Thought*, writes:

> Chairs are continuous with floors and walls, but without the least hesitation we discriminate parts of the chair from the floor with which it is continuous and group them into one thing .... Indeed, there are writers who would say that utility is the sole ground for selecting any set of qualities as essential to any object. 'The only meaning of essence is teleological,' James wrote.[5]

Husserl's conception of intentionality can be clarified further by distinguishing it from the traditions of Brentano on the one side and psychologism on the other. Husserl was not an idealist in the strict sense; but to see his close association with idealist doctrines prevents certain misinterpretations of his views. Brentano's theory of intentionality existed within a realistic metaphysics. The "look," according to Brentano, is to the external world. Psychologism, on the other hand, tends to end in subjectivism, which Husserl likewise denies. Husserl's version of intentionality can best be understood by considering it within the metaphysical framework of absolute or objective idealism. Husserl feels that he has transcended the realism-idealism dispute. His conclusions resemble but his methods differ from those of positivism, the analysis of ordinary language, and pragmatism.

---

[1] Alfred North Whitehead, *Process and Reality* (New York: The Macmillan Co., Inc., 1929), p. 68.
[2] Henri Bergson, *Creative Evolution*, trans. A. Mitchell (New York: Henry Holt & Co., 1911), p. 157.
[3] *Ibid.*, p. 186.
[4] *Ibid.*, p. 302.
[5] Brand Blanshard, *The Nature of Thought*, Vol. I (London: George Allen and Unwin, Ltd., 1939), p. 130.

Husserl prefers the name "intentionality" — and eventually "constitution" — to designate this active participation of the ego in the structuring of our experience.

The concept of intentionality is already present in the classical and realistic philosophies of Plato and Aquinas.[1] To recognize the presence of intentionality is to realize the difference between, on the one hand, the act and the operation of thought, and, on the other, the object which this thought "intends." Thus, we must not confuse the characteristics of the psychological, temporal, language-bound, and otherwise contingent process of counting with the properties of the atemporal product of that process, such as *number*, which is indepentent of language and other contingencies. And thus, in general, to every mental act (intentional act), whether veridical or not, corresponds an object (intentional object) whose properties are different from those of the constituting act. The separation here alluded to is meant neither as an inference nor as a logical necessity; rather, it is the result of careful introspective empirical investigation.

A metaphor might help illustrate the nature of intentionality. Imagine a skyscraper in the night upon which numerous colored searchlights, imitating a mosaic, cast the piebald image of a faun. The object of perception, the cogitatum, is a colorful faun. The faun is evidently an intention; it is something meant, intended, constituted, designed. The faun is not something "objective" in the sense that the skyscraper might be thought to be. In order to understand fully the object of perception we must focus our attention and analysis on the luminous streams, that is, on the *cogitationes* themselves.

This metaphor is not meant to demonstrate the validity of the doctrine of intentions: only to illustrate it. The question of evidence is a separate one, to which we must now turn.

Intentionality is the structure of consciousness *per se*. When, through the repeated exercise of the phenomenological epoche (and eventually through other reductions), consciousness has been stripped of all contingent and accidental characteristics and the essence of consciousness emerges in its pristine purity, then we recognize that consciousness is a pure stream, a mere "look,"

---

[1] *Cf.* John Wild, "Husserl's Critique of Psychologism," in Farber, ed., *op. cit.*, pp. 23–24.

a radiation of "transcendence" from an ego-pole to cogitata. Intentionality is the fundamental category of being. All being, *i.e.*, all experience, has a common and discernible characteristic; and that trait can be best designated and described by calling it a pure "look." The structure of this universal and pure "look" is encapsuled in Husserl's descriptive tripartite formula, *"ego cogito cogitatum."* The truth of this assertion can be verified by careful analysis of one's own experience, by what Husserl sometimes terms "philosophical self-disclosure and self-examination," or, to continue with the Cartesian parallelism, by concerted self-conscious meditation. This type of verification shares many important elements with the empirical method of the sciences. The difference lies in subject-matter.

(ii) Evidence for Intentionality. It will be practical, for purposes of exposition, to classify the various types of evidence for the existence of intentionality into five groups: (1) immediate evidence; (2) unity of objects in space; (3) unity of objects in time; (4) unity of the observing ego; (5) the possibility of error. Each one must be presented in some detail.

(1) If we take seriously Husserl's method of the phenomenological epoche, and if phenomenological researches do in fact yield the ubiquitous intentionality of experience, it follows that intentionality should be subject to direct apprehension and inspection. The intentionality of experience emerges when we apply the epoche to the *cogito*, the *act* of experiencing. This focus is established when our attention oscillates between the complete object perceived and the act of perception. This type of evidence is indeed vague, and, if it can be recognized, would of itself hardly suffice to establish the existence, and much less the importance, of intentionality.

(2) One of the most striking aspects of experience is the contraposition of the object as a unit with the obviously multifarious ways in which it appears. Husserl uses a hexahedron as example. A hexahedron may be a shiny silver die with black spots. Even cursory analysis discloses that my conception of it as one, unchanging, solid, cubic, and monochromatic object differs from my actual perception of it as a multiplicity of changing shapes and impressions. The relation between the believed object and the actual presentations from which it

emerges is one of the major problems in epistemology. It seems evident that the cohesion of the multiple perceptions in "one" object may quite properly be referred to, as Husserl does, as an instance of egological constitution.

For example, that the angles of the die are all right angles, at one and the same time, is a belief or an inference, not an immediate sensory experience. Only rarely do they appear as right angles to the eye; most of the time they are likely to appear acute or obtuse. And of course I never see all angles at one time. The belief that the die is "in reality" a cube is of the order of an ideal, a metaphor, a construct, or, in a sense, a convention. The warrant for the convention is, in all probability, its practical import. This has been a pragmatic contention of long standing.

Kant's example of a house is another one which gives evidence for the view that what we experience is not merely "there," "before us," but is constituted and intended by us. I conceive of a house as *one* object, whose parts have specific and invariant geometric relationships. This unity of relationships is inferred or constructed; it is not given in immediate experience. I perceive only one room at a time — and only one part of it, and a distorted one at that. My total visual record of the house that I have just inspected is akin to the succession of frames on a film. The frames are "adjacent." It requires an act of subjective synthesis to reconstruct them into the "real" house, which turns out to be more a conceptual object than a perceived one.

It must never be forgotten, of course, that the intention is rarely conscious: it is automatic, passive, unconscious, and anonymous. Husserl refers to the ego's constitution of the world as a passive genesis. Yet the facts of experience make the postulation of intentionality necessary. The voluntaristic connotations of the terms "constitution" and "intentionality" are perhaps unfortunate and misleading.

(3) A perception, even if it is continuous and unchanging, is nonetheless composite in that it is made up of time intervals. Two appearances may be similar in all respects; but the fact that they are apprehended at different times means that their unity is also a matter of subjective decision, constitution, and intention, not of pure givenness. To ascribe both of the appearances that occur at different intervals in time to one and the same object

is an act of subjective synthesis. An object is not merely what we synthesize it to be within the rather narrow stretch of the present, but we add to our present experiences of an object the reminiscences of the past and the anticipations of the future. An object is not only its present: it carries a past with it (Sartre maintains, for example, that to desire an object is to desire its past). Above all, an object is what it is in virtue of predictions that we make about its behavior in the future. This totality of past, present, and future coheres as one object through an act of egological constitution, through an intention.

The following example might clarify the point. I perceive a doorknob at this moment. The doorknob is not a diaphanous apparition but an intentional object. Part of the meaning of this particular doorknob is that it has been there for a long time, and that it will continue to be there. I make the tacit prediction that, if I touch it, the doorknob would feel hard and enable me to open the door. I further predict that any other individual under the same circumstances will make similar predictions, and I believe that both mine and his predictions will be confirmed. The predictions submerged within the intentional object parallel those of scientific theories. An object is thus a microscopic scientific theory. The combination of past, present, and future is synthesized into one intended construct, which is the "object." One of the many names that Husserl gives to this constitutive agent in experience is the "synthetic consciousness."

(4) More pervasive than any particular objective unity is the unity of the perceiver. Kant referred to a similar aspect of constitution as the transcendental unity of apperception. Husserl refers to it, somewhat ambiguously, as the transcendental Ego. We have a multiplicity of experiences in space and time. Not only are these multiplicities organized into specific and individual objects, but the totality of that experience is organized into *one* totality, and finally into one totality that is perceived by one continuous ego. The unity of the ego is interrupted by sleep, split by memory-lapses, shredded by the spacio-temporal flux, and torn by conflicting values, loyalties, attitudes, and emotions. In the face of these pulverizing threats the ego retains its unremitting sense of unity and integrity. This unity of the

ego is one of the most fundamental acts of constitution, and hence of intentionality.

(5) The last class of evidence that can be brought to bear on the existence of intentionality is the possibility of error. In all our experiences there is a core about which we cannot be mistaken. But that about which we could possibly be mistaken — even if it requires the postulation of such an outrageous hypothesis as that of Descartes' demon — "as powerful as he is malevolent" — must be our own contribution to experience. That about which we can be mistaken is a belief, an inference, a proposition, a construction, in short, an intention. The only hypothesis that makes sense of the various aspects of the element of error in experience is the postulation of intentionality.

A possible confusion arises at this point in Husserl's thought. On the one hand, intentionality, as the process of construction, is that in experience about which we can be mistaken, and on the other, the phenomenological epoche, which discloses the presence of intentionality, means to exclude, by bracketing, precisely that about which we can be mistaken, *i.e.*, that which is not purely given. It would follow that the epoche, by definition, brackets out intentionality. But if intentionality is discovered and then examined by focusing the phenomenological method on it, that is, by bracketing all that is not given in pure experience, then we will have excluded intentionality itself by bracketing it away. Intentionality and the phenomenological epoche appear to be contradictory notions; it seems logically impossible ever to focus phenomenological attention on intentionality. This is a serious problem, but, given a few *ad hoc* hypotheses, can be resolved satisfactorily.

The epoche can variously be applied to levels of experience: experience comes in degrees of complexity and levels of organization. That about which I cannot be mistaken (such as is illustrated by the traditional examples of color patches, variable shapes, etc.) is part of my total experience, and I can study that part by concentrating the phenomenological epoche on it. However, exploring experience with the criterion "that about which I cannot be mistaken" does not yield exclusively and uniformly one type of data. It is possible for me *not-to-be-mistaken* about the presentational structure of inferences as well as about that of simpler appearances, such as sense data. My interpretation of pure sense data is in turn a pure experience, an original sense datum in its own right. That is to say, interpretations, constructions, and inferences, *i.e.*, intentions, have their own presentational manifestation and structure. There is something in the presentation of an inference, construction, or intention about which I cannot be mistaken. Here we have what might appropriately be termed a "second-level" presentation. I can further make inferences on the basis of these second-level interpretations; I can develop constructs out of these and manipulate them through intentionality. The case has an analogy in the human organism: cells are combined to construct individual organs, organs are combined into a human body, human bodies are combined into families, and then societies, nations, and so forth. At all levels but the lowest, these organizations can be "mistaken," that is, morbid, uncooperative, ineffectual, and impractical. For example, the liver, that is, a total organism, may be malfunctioning (which corresponds to mistaken interpretation), whereas its component cells (which correspond to that about which I cannot be mistaken) might individually be normal and healthy. At a higher level of analysis, however, I cannot be mistaken about the structure of this malfunction of the liver, and similarly, I cannot be mistaken about the fact and structure of my particular interpretations (which may be misinterpretations) of sensa.

The semantic notion of meta-languages may profitably be applied to the philosophy of experience. I cannot be mistaken about an experience *qua* experience. A meta-experience is, by analogy, an experience or statement about that experience: the reference might not correspond to the facts, and here I can be mistaken. The lower-level epoche brackets the experience through the process of excluding the meta-experience. The same type of analysis can now be applied to the meta-experience. A higher-level epoche brackets the meta-experience by excluding meta-meta-experiences, that is, by excluding experiences, statements, beliefs, and constructs about these meta-experiences. In this way it is possible to focus on intentionality, where intentionality is the pure, uninterpreted presentation of the manner in which I interpret and organize my experience. Intentionality is a meta-experience. In order to focus on this meta-experience we must bracket meta-meta-experiences. Of course, the notions of "experience" and "meta-experience," as is true of the parallel notions "language" and "meta-language," are relative. Their significance rests on the relation they have to each other and not on some absolute referent to which they point. Experiences, even of a high level of complexity and organization, have their own unique and discernible presentational characteristics. The description of these characteristics, central to which is intentionality, is the task of phenomenology.

In conclusion, the following summary definitions must be borne in mind. The *cogitationes* are the constitutive acts, that is, the acts that create intentional objects. Sometimes Husserl identifies intentionality with the traditional notion of the a priori. The *cogitata* are the objects corresponding to these constitutive acts. These objects are often referred to as "indices," and they are of many types. These objects can be physical and perceptual things; but they can also be *ideal objects*, sometimes called "the indices of constitutive systems." Among these ideal objects Husserl lists ideas, conceptions of the nature of the world, propositions, inferences, proofs, theories, and truths.

(iii) Further Exposition of Intentionality. (1) An important concept in understanding the structure of intentionality is that of "horizons." There are significant similarities between Husserl's notion of horizons and the concepts of potentiality or dispositional properties, and also with William James' notion of "fringes" in the stream of thought.[1] Husserl's position is, in effect, that potentiality is an aspect of the experience of any object. The potentiality of sugar to dissolve in water is, in a real sense, part of the total experience associated with the object "sugar." The dispositional properties of objects have their own unique and discernible presentational structure, which is a mixture of remembrances and anticipations. I remember seeing sugar dissolve in liquids; I remember reading about the molecular interactions involved, and I anticipate that my tacit predictions, based on past experience, will be confirmed.

---

[1] For an interesting parallelism between Husserl and James see Herbert Spiegelberg, *op. cit.*, pp. 111–117.

These are all items in my apprehension of sugar. Since Husserl uses the expanded conception of experience typical of idealistic philosophies, it is easy to see how he can, in effect, maintain that potentialities are given as pure data of experience. In order to focus on potentialities, the total object with its manifold implications must be bracketed, not merely what is narrowly referred to as its sense data. The potentialities that comprise the tangential and circumscribed structure of an object constitute its horizon.

Horizons, which appear in every *cogito*, have thus the following characteristics. (a) The act of perception or experience comprises expectations of things other than what is ordinarily referred to as immediate presentations. (b) The perception of objects also involves associations with past events: a "mnemonic mass," as Blanshard calls it, accompanies every *cogito* or act of perception. The meaning of an object is winnowed from its antecedent mnemonic mass and its anticipated confirmed predictions. (c) I need horizons to clarify the intention of objective reference. Unless I am clear about the horizons involved in perception, the object that I intend in my experience is incomplete. If we look upon sense data as two-dimensional, we can say that horizons add depth to the perception: they add the third dimension.

(2) The object or *cogitatum* serves as "index" in the exploration of intentionality. The object serves as anchor for the fluid and constantly moving and changing total intention. If we wish to analyze the nature of the intention — the synthesizing, constituting, and structuring *cogito* — we must view the *cogitatum* as a clue to the structure of the *cogito*. The horizons come to a focus in the *cogitatum*. The acts make up the *cogito*; intentionality, the subjective and synthetic act of constituting the *cogitatum*, can be explored only if we use the *cogitatum* as our base of operations. The *cogitatum* is the source of our information about horizons and intentions, just as a periscope is the source of our information about the submarine beneath. For purposes of exposition, as should be evident by now, we must distinguish between a complete and a simplified *cogitatum*. The simplified *cogitatum* is the narrow and two-dimensional complex of sense data. The complete *cogitatum* is the total object, which includes the horizons, that is, intentions, of the *cogito*. Husserl is not

always either clear or consistent in his use of *"cogitatum."*
Sometimes, and in one and the same context, the *cogitatum* is
more comprehensive in its reference than at other times. Part
of the fault lies in the fact that a precise and logical analysis of
vague, shifting, and irrational experience is impossible.

The *cogito,* whose exploration begins with the simplified
cogitatum, is like a flux with no clear limits: it extends indefinitely
into the future and into the past, and in all directions into space.
However, the flux is not quite as desultory and chaotic as these
statements suggest. The flux follows certain general patterns
and laws, and phenomenology seeks to discover these. The
process of discovering and describing these laws is in fact describing what Husserl calls "transcendental consciousness" (see
section *c*). It is the transcendental consciousness which creates
these meanings and intentions.

(3) The notion of universe or "world" has a special place in
Husserl's presentation and analysis of intentionality. The world,
that is, the totality of being, is experienced as a whole, a unity.
But the unity of the world is unique. The world, as we experience
it, is not delimited by an outside. Husserl's concern with "world"
is related to the general problem of being, a problem which today
has assumed special importance in the writings of most existentialists. For example, the problem of being is the underlying
theme in the work of Heidegger. In Jaspers' philosophy, the
traditional notion of being reappears under the name of "the
comprehensive" (*das Umgreifende*). It therefore becomes a
matter of special importance to focus, in the sense of a *cogitatum,*
on the world as a whole, and then analyze the structure of the
particular *cogito* that constitutes such rather extraordinary
object. The analysis will disclose the a priori principles, characteristics, and laws which, for rationalistic philosophies, govern
the world. One intentional structure of the world is best described
by the term "infinity." "Infinity" is not meant in a strict mathematical or logical sense, but as a metaphor, as a descriptive term
designating the endlessness and the openness of our experience
when it is focused on the world itself. Husserl later — in *Die
Krise der europäischen Wissenschaften und die transzendentale
Phänomenologie (The Crisis of the European Sciences and Transcendental Phenomenology)* — has dealt more extensively with this

problem and developed the now famous and more restricted notion of *Lebenswelt*.

(4) Husserl deals in some detail with the nature of evidence. Since contemporary analytic philosophy concerns itself with criteria of cognitive significance, that is, with the problems of confirmation and verification and their relation to meaning, some important coincidences of interest and subject matter between analytic philosophy and phenomenology suggest themselves.

Husserl holds the view that evidence, as all other *cogitata*, is an intention. This point is not altogether clear, even though Husserl manifestly distinguishes the experience of the *fact of certainty* from the experience of the *feeling of certainty*. Fact and feeling differ from each other; the former is objective and the latter subjective. However, both fact and feeling are presentations, that is, experiences, and are thus constituted, although differently, in, by, and through subjectivity. He may mean a number of things. For one, some objects in experience appear in the mode or character of *objective certainty* and *conviction*. This mode of presentation characterizes mathematical laws, objects, and operations. To this extent it may be quite legitimate to describe the phenomenological presentation of analytic truths in terms of their element of conviction. But modern logicians have also pointed out the non-empirical, arbitrary, and even conventional nature of mathematical truths. To the degree that mathematical truths are conventional, that is, to the degree that they depend on the arbitrary selection of certain primitive postulates or axioms, primitive definitions, and rules of procedure, they clearly and actively (rather than passively) are intentional and constitutive. In modern logic, where we find numerous artificial or ideal languages, these certainties are constituted not anonymously or automatically, but consciously and deliberately. But this is not the place to work out the many facets and problems of the nature of evidence.

But Husserl's conception of evidence as an intention goes far beyond its application to the question of mathematical certainty. When Husserl writes that evidence, as a *cogitatum*, is constituted by the transcendental Ego, he does not mean that evidence is subjective. Whether p is evidence for q is not a matter of decision. Nor is the occurrence of p a subjective act. However, as the analysis of Hume's views about the problem of induction has shown, there is no proof for induction; induction is simply what we *mean* by evidence. The meaning of evidence is arbitrary in the sense that the truth it discloses is not to be interpreted in terms of a correspondence theory of truth; its meaning is discovered, however, in terms of a pragmatic theory of truth, in that to accept induction as the meaning of evidence is more "practical" than to reject it. The same applies to Husserl's analysis of evidence as being intentional. The evidence is not subjectively provided, invented, or constituted; it is discovered — in laboratories or through other sources of observation. What is subjectively constituted is the meaning and the nature of evidence itself. The concept of evidence is a subjective projection. Evidence is not the kind of thing we find in the world: it is not like a patch of color or a shape. Evidence is an interpretation of what we find in the world; and, as an interpretation, evidence is a theoretical construct — *i.e.*, an intention — derived from the pure *cogitata* of experience. And as such, the meaning of evidence is constituted with "practical" ends in view.

Husserl's analysis of evidence as an intentional structure proceeds along pragmatic and positivistic lines, even though his terminology tends to obscure this relationship. He agrees with pragmatism when he says that by "evidence" we mean or intend confirmation or disconfirmation of prior predictions. Furthermore, he holds that the meaning of evidence depends on certain procedures which will determine whether evidence exists or not; here the analogy to the method of science and the positivist meaning criterion is evident. These procedures are subjectively constituted to fulfill certain subjectively established goals, such as knowledge or technology. He writes, "one can always ask what the procedures are that decide whether an object is real or illusory" (p. 22).

Finally, empirical evidence is constituted as progressive, that is to say, it results in probability, not certainty: prediction (*i.e.*, horizons) are theoretically infinite, and their full verification does not take place until all of them have been tested. Verification is thus restricted to probable confirmation. The procedures that define evidence are the creations of my own subjectivity, which, in the last analysis, is the transcendental Ego. Husserl writes, "these confirmation-procedures ... belong to me as transcendental subjectivity and make sense only a such" (p. 23).

The meaning of evidence, as suggested earlier, is not always constituted deliberately and freely: it is rather discovered by me to be constituted anonymously.

(5) Corollary to Husserl's views on evidence are his views on reality and truth. Husserl writes, "existence and essence have for us no other meaning in reality and truth than that of possible confirmation." This positivistic and pragmatic attitude is followed a little later by the statement, *"true being ... has significance only as a particular correlate of my own intentionality"* [italics his] (p. 23). For Husserl, as for the positivists, reality, essence, and meaning are synonymous with confirmability.

As a matter of fact, Husserl recognized his links with pragmatism and positivism — manifested in the joint tenure of the empirical attitude and the confirmation theory of meaning — when he writes, in his *Ideen* I, "It is we who are the genuine positivists." [1]

Husserl tends to refer to these pervasive and fundamental aspects of intentionality as "constitutive problems." These problems include the constitution of mind and matter, reason and reality, consciousness and true being, as well as the existence of an external world. These fundamental aspects of existence, experience, and the world are not to be viewed as absolute and objective facts, but rather as constitutions, intentions, organizations that human subjectivity — as the transcendental Ego — effects, both deliberately and anonymously. These entities are culled from the pure qualia of our experience and transformed according to certain "a priori" laws.

Husserl's view of constitution is reminiscent not only of both XIXth and XXth century positivism, but also of Kant and the entire post-Kantian idealistic movement of the Nineteenth Century. For these philosophers, Fichte, Hegel, Schopenhauer, Schelling, Royce, and others, including the romantic post-Kantians, the transcendental Ego creates its opposite — the world or nature — for the purpose of its own self-conscious self-realization. Husserl's view does not possess the romantic, aesthetic, and mystical overtones of some of his predecessors; he

---

[1] *Cf.* Herbert Spiegelberg, *op. cit.*, p. 130.

is interested in cold, pure, and scientific epistemological issues. But in the matter of intentionality and constitution, Husserl's cultural dependence on the German tradition that preceded him is apparent.

Furthermore, Husserl maintains that reason itself can be viewed as a cogitatum, with its own, particular, and unique intentional structure. Reason is one mode of subjectivity; it is a peculiar mode of projection.

Existentialism has been accused of irrationalism. There is some foundation for this accusation. Following Husserl's view that reason itself is constituted by the transcendental Ego, some existentialists maintain that scientific, mathematical, logical, and other rational pursuits are particular projects of man, suited for particular ends, but which do not necessarily embody the objectivity and absoluteness that we like to attribute to these cognitive approaches to the world. This existentialist view parallels Bergson's distinction between the intellect, which is mathematical and practical, and intuition, which according to him is the only authentic approach to reality. The view that reason itself is produced through an act of constitution has its parallel in Schopenhauer, for whom rational thought, which is bound by the fourfold root of the principle of sufficient reason, is a purely practical approach to reality. To him, reason is the mind governed by the will to live, the mind put to the service of the desire for survival. In Dewey's conception of intelligence as an instrument for problem solving and biological survival we find another parallel to Husserl's view of the intentional constitution of reason.

The most important, and also most puzzling, constituted *cogitatum* is the ego itself. The ego constitutes itself. Husserl was wise in pointing out that this is "the most radical constitutive problem." The contemporary Polish phenomenologist and friend of Husserl, Roman Ingarden, emphasized the paradox of Husserl's position, which is that the *constituted* ego is also the *agent* of its own constitution. A possible solution to what in effect is a conundrum can be found in Husserl's implicit conception of the levels of the ego. The ego is, first of all, a center from which the cogitationes radiate. This center is the ultimate ego-pole, the ultimate source of subjectivity. It is the transcendental Ego.

As mentioned earlier, in Oriental philosophy this source is referred to as the Atman or Purusha, and has important religious significance. But also, the ego is a center of convictions and habits. This may be called (although Husserl does not do so in these lectures) the psychological or the empirical ego.

Finally, Husserl refers to the laws governing the intentional structure of constitutions as the inborn a priori. Husserl writes that *"the ego ... possesses a tremendous inborn a priori"* [italics his] (p. 28). We discover the a priori when we observe the acts of apprehension, the *cogitationes*, and the laws governing their operations. This notion of the a priori is pre-eminently Kantian. The a priori consists of that part of the human mind which embodies the pure forms of intuition (space and time) and the pure concepts (the categories). All experience is organized in terms of these prior demands.

(6) The fundamental epistemological problem of the existence of an external world is that of transcendence. How is it possible for the ego to make true assertions about that which is beyond immediate experience? How can the ego reach out, beyond the senses, and perhaps even beyond reason, to the real and permanent world outside? What is the nature of the world independently of being perceived? Husserl follows what was in fact Dewey's recommendation that philosophic problems are not to be answered in terms of the alternatives that the questions themselves suggest. Pragmatism, positivism, and the philosophies of linguistic analysis have taken this advice, and it has affected their analysis and solution of the problem of the existence and nature of the external world. Husserl, in a manner similar to that of these philosophies now prevailing in England and America, contends that the problem arises only within the natural, straightforward, or engaged attitude. It arises in pre-philosophic reflection. The phenomenological epoche brackets this problem, and it is never reintroduced. The philosophic error has been to handle this problem in terms of the non-philosophic concepts and categories developed within the natural attitude. The language used to handle the problem of transcendence was developed for restricted "natural" and "straightforward" uses only; applying that language beyond its legitimate realm leads to puzzles, contradiction, and spurious problems.

The difference between Husserl's treatment of the problem and that of the philosophies of analysis is that the former is an investigation of the phenomena of experience as these introduce the problem of the existence of an external world, whereas the latter restrict themselves to linguistic investigations and analyses of how the functioning of language leads to these epistemological puzzles.

The distinctions essential to the articulation of the problem of transcendence itself, such as the contrasts of veridical and illusory experiences, mind and matter, appearance and reality, truth and falsity, even subjectivity and objectivity, occur within consciousness itself, are concepts that make sense only within the confines of conscious phenomena. These insights were developed already by Berkeley and Kant.

Given the egocentric predicament, Husserl's problem becomes how to achieve *objective* certainty. This question, according to Husserl, is a meaningless or contradictory problem. The mistake is that I think of the ego — which is really the transcendental Ego — as having an exterior. The transcendental Ego, in other words, the totality of my consciousness, is just not the kind of thing that has an exterior. There can be no exterior to it either in thought or in actual experience. The epistemological problem arises through this error; but the phenomenological epoche eliminates this pseudo-externality. Husserl's idealistic leanings, which become very pronounced in his later works such as the *Pariser Vorträge* and *Cartesianische Meditationen*, are already illustrated in his conception of the transcendental Ego and his attitude towards the problem of the existence of an external world.

Ultimately Husserl must and does admit that transcendence itself, as a mode of being, is an intention in turn and has its own and discoverable egological constitution. The consequences of this admission are not worked out.

The difference between phenomenological and traditional epistemology becomes thus quite clear. Traditional epistemology deals with the arguments for the existence of the putative immanence-transcendence dichotomy, and proposes presumptive solutions. Phenomenological epistemology, however, is a systematic description and analysis of the uninterpreted act of cognition

as the latter presents itself in consciousness. Progress in epistemology is predicated on this latter, empirical, approach.

(c) *The Transcendental Ego and the Theory of Reductions*. This
section expands the discussion of the epoche by focusing on
what is, after intentionality, perhaps the most significant result
of phenomenological investigations. Through a series of operations that Husserl terms the "transcendental-phenomenological
reduction" — which is really no more than an extended application of the phenomenological epoche — he reaches, in the
transcendental Ego, what he claims to be the source of being,
of objectivity, of reality, and of truth. In his earlier works, such
as the *Logische Untersuchungen* and the *Formale und transzendentale Logik (Formal and Transcendental Logic)*, Husserl was
concerned principally with the bracketing and subsequent
intuitive examination (*Aufweis*) of essences (*Wesensschau*)
or universal concepts. Later, especially in the *Cartesianische
Meditationen*, the focus of Husserl's interest turns to the
transcendental Ego. The expansion of the epoche through
further reductions corresponds to this shift of interest and
emphasis. Unfortunately, the *Pariser Vorträge* offer only desultory and incomplete accounts of the very difficult concepts of
"reduction" and "transcendental Ego." These insights matured
slowly in Husserl's thought and, in particular regarding the
transcendental Ego, did not receive the serious attention from
his followers that Husserl thought was needed and deserved.
The question of his successor in Freiburg was related to this
problem. Alexander Pfänder was a serious candidate in Husserl's
mind until the former refused to follow Husserl in the more esoteric and idealistic-oriented aspects of the theory of reductions.
A similar situation arose in Husserl's final designation of Heidegger as his successor, and his later disappointment and
bitterness over the latter's philosophical heterodoxy with respect
to the transcendental Ego and other matters.[1]

The present exposition, which goes beyond the material found
in these lectures, is necessary for a comprehensive understanding
and appreciation of Husserl's contribution to philosophy and
his place in history. This section proposes to show precisely how
the phenomenological reductions lead to an apprehension of the
transcendental Ego.

Husserl writes that "I am the sole source" and have total responsibility for the "logical justification" of any and all beliefs. This means that the ultimate source or nature of subjectivity, namely the transcendental Ego, is the metaphysical ground of all being, the epistemological ground of all truth and knowledge, and also — here emerges the existentialist contribution to contemporary philosophy — the axiological ground for all responsible and free choices.

The transcendental Ego leads to a stoic, Kantian, and Sartrean sense of autonomy and responsibility in ethics as well as in ontology. The highest appeal to which I have recourse is my very own subjectivity.

Following both idealistic and Cartesian lines, Husserl holds that the being of the world presupposes the existence of my pure Ego. It is this position that needs clarification.

Husserl's conception of the transcendental Ego, although not envisioned by him as such, can be understood as an outgrowth of the Nineteenth-Century objective or absolute idealism of men like Hegel, Schelling, Schlegel, Fichte, Schopenhauer, and has substantial parallels to the idealistic philosophy of Josiah Royce, with the latter's emphasis on community in addition to the other characteristics of objective idealism. In fact, the term "phenomenology" was used first by Hegel. The notion of "transcendental" acts, principles, categories, and events stems from the father of Nineteenth-Century objective idealism, Immanuel Kant. A second precursor of the transcendental Ego is the objective idealism prevalent in Oriental philosophy. Husserl does not acknowledge and probably was not aware of the profound similarity between his view of the transcendental Ego and such famous Sanskrit formulas as "tat twam asi" (that art thou), "the Atman is the Brahman," as well as the relations between the Atman and the jiva, and between Purusha and prakriti. It is doubtful that Oriental philosophy influenced Husserl directly — or even indirectly through Schopenhauer. Nonetheless, acquaintance with Oriental philosophy — a topic that is of increasing interest to Western philosophy — is a good introduction to the understanding of the transcendental Ego. It is far from being a case of inverse chauvinism to aver that the analyses of the transcendental Ego, especially as found in the systems of orthodox Hindu thought that go under the names of Vedanta and Sankhya, are far more trenchant and sophisticated than those of Husserl, although they do lack some of his epistemological refinements.

Through the reductions Husserl hopes to disclose the pure subject, the "I" that stands behind all appearances as their observer and behind all free acts as their agent. His is the problem, at its deepest level, of the self. The ego, however, is not an inferred entity, a substance, but one aspect of or a locus in my experience of the world. Husserl's analysis of the ego is strictly empirical. In searching for the self, he examines the data of immediate experience: he asks, in effect, How do I feel, what do I experience, when I say with the God of the Old Testament, "I am who am"?

As much as Husserl's later philosophical position points to idealism, important differences remain. The difference between Husserl's phenomenology and objective idealism can be characterized in a fourfold manner. First, Husserl emphasizes methodology and de-emphasizes metaphysics. The reverse is true of objective idealism. Nonetheless, Husserl's doctrine of the transcendental Ego is indeed a close approximation to a metaphysical theory. Second, Husserl's empirical spirit and rigor are not typical of idealistic philosophies. Thus, the difference between phenomenology and objective idealism is not as much in spirit — where there are important affinities — as it is in the method of scientific meticulousness, analysis, and precision.

Third, for Husserl, in contradistinction to objective idealism, consciousness is no "primal stuff." In general, consciousness itself is bracketed in the phenomenological explorations of the Ego. Consciousness cannot serve as the root metaphor or original substance in terms of which all of existence is to be interpreted because "consciousness" is then used in a transcendental sense. A term has meaning only through negation. To define a term involves, in part, to indicate what it is not. "Consciousness," to have any meaning, presupposes the possibility of the nonconscious (traditionally matter or nature). In short, idealism presupposes the meaning and the possible existence of non-ideational matter. When Husserl focuses on the pure Ego he brackets consciousness. All that remains in experience is the pure intentional look.

To bracket consciousness implies (i) that consciousness has *meaning*, since the epoche discloses a residue — the transcendental Ego — which is neither consciousness nor non-consciousness, but which is the ego that *observes* consciousness as it would any *cogitatum*, and (ii) that, contrary to traditional idealism, consciousness is not the stuff out of which all of being is fashioned. If we use "consciousness" in the same transcendental way in which idealism does, in which case the term "consciousness" is coextensive with the terms "being," "everything," and "universe," then the term is really quite pointless and might as well be abandoned altogether. This is a subtle and important distinction between any kind of idealism and Husserl's later phenomenology.

Finally, Husserl's phenomenological position strictly eschews the solipsism that is consequent to the egocentric predicament, and which is a characteristic danger of subjective idealism. The psychological or empirical ego — that is, the passing stream of an individual consciousness — is not to be identified with the observer behind this stream, *i.e.*, the transcendental Ego. The empirical ego is merely one item within the totality of empirical presentations before me. Other items within that total presentation are such events as my body and other selves. Husserl avoids solipsism by holding that my psychological states, perceptions, attitudes, emotions, in sum, my person, are all *cogitata* or objects in the intentional look of the much more fundamental transcendental Ego.

After calling attention to some differences between Husserl's position and traditional idealisms, we can proceed to an exposition of the transcendental Ego proper.

The following is an attempt at a clear and accurate account of Husserl's conception of the transcendental Ego. However, the terms of exposition are not Husserl's, and consequently this material constitutes in great measure an interpretation.

The careful and unprejudiced phenomenological and empirical description of being as it presents itself to us leads to an altogether new and heterodox set of categories. Traditional categories, such as mind and matter, space and time, subject and object, inner and outer experience, man and world, and the like, involve unwarranted assumptions, inferences, and interpretations. Contemporary philosophical analyses, by Wittgenstein, Ryle, Heidegger, and Merleau-Ponty, to name but a few — in both the language- and the experience-oriented methodologies — have demonstrated that these categories break down when scrutinized. In order to understand Husserl, a new set of categories must be developed; these are to be empirical, confirmable, and ubiquitous traits of experience.

First, a name is needed to designate the totality of experience. The term "universe" suggests itself, but its connotations reintroduce, without examination, the epistemological problem of the existence of an external world. The name for the totality of experience should reflect the empirically observable characteristic that all experiences and facts which appear real and meaningful are related to me. This pervasive relation that meaningful being has to me can be stressed by naming the totality of possible experience or of being "transcendental consciousness," or perhaps the "transcendental Realm." The adjective "transcendental" emphasizes that the trait applies to all experience, whereas the noun "consciousness" points to the experienced fact that all being is related to me in some way. We must now explore phenomenologically the contents of transcendental consciousness and discover some of its general traits. This ontological analysis precedes any such distinctions as those between my ego and that of others, and between my ego and the world.

I can identify classes of objects within the matrix or continuum of "transcendental consciousness." There are physical objects, conceptual objects, icons or imaginary objects, affective objects, and other selves. Anything that becomes "an object of consciousness" is *ipso facto* discovered within this realm of transcendental consciousness. There are two items of particular importance within this transcendental realm. These are my physical body and my psychological or empirical self. I tend to identify my "true, inner self or ego" with either my body or my passing psychological states. A common term for the totality of my psychological states, dispositions, feelings, anticipations, and attitudes is that of "person." It is fundamental to an understanding of the transcendental Ego to realize that what

we ordinarily mean by "me," by "I," by "myself," by "my ego,"
is really merely one of many *objects* within the totality of experience here termed "transcendental consciousness."

At the "center" of transcendental consciousness we experience
the peculiar and unique existence of an "I-pole," a core from
which all intentional streams of experience radiate. Although
this core itself can never be made objective, it is nonetheless
present in experience. This core, which is a distinct and ubiquitous aspect of all my experience, is the perennial observer of
anything within transcendental consciousness or the transcendental realm. This I-pole, the *terminus a quo* of all experience,
is ever-present, yet cannot be apprehended in the normal way
in which objects are apprehended because the disclosure of this
I-pole contravenes the characteristic intentional structure of
consciousness. This I-pole is the transcendental Ego or the
transcendental subject. In the strictest sense, I am that I-pole.
I am the transcendental subject. One of the important aspects
of being human is that I tend to identify the transcendental
subject with two items that are really *objects* to the "impartial
observer," as Husserl often calls the transcendental Ego. These
objects are my body and my person. We may refer to either or
both of these objects as the psychological or empirical self. The
"real me," the transcendental Ego, is not to be identified with
only one person among millions. All persons, including me, are
within purview of the transcendental Ego, although it is nonetheless true that the relation between my person and the transcendental Ego differs in fundamental respects from the relation
other selves have to the one transcendental Ego with which I am
acquainted.

The transcendental Ego is not only passive, as Husserl seems
to emphasize, but also active. In numerous instances I experience myself as agent or creator. In these cases, the transcendental Ego is experienced not merely as an observer or spectator,
but as a spontaneous initiator as well.

Although Husserl's conception of the transcendental Ego
comes close to the predecing one, he often seems to mean by it
either the intentional stream that flows between the transcendental subject and items within transcendental consciousness,
or pure transcendental consciousness itself.

The distinction between the transcendental Ego and the psychological ego is not new. In Vedanta, as mentioned earlier, this distinction is embodied in the relation between the Atman and the jiva. William James alludes to a similar distinction in the first volume of his *Principles of Psychology*. In much of Western objective idealism, however, this distinction is quite obscure; at best it is latent.

A helpful descriptive term used by Husserl — and also by Hegel and Sartre — to designate the transcendental Ego is that the Ego is "being for itself." In other words, the essential descriptive trait of self-consciousness can be recorded by stating that self-consciousness is a unique type of being, namely, being that is for itself rather than merely in itself. This similarity between Husserl and Sartre may assist the understanding of Husserl, but it must not mislead us into formulating a closer affinity between Sartre and Husserl than in fact obtains. The transcendental Ego, for Sartre, is simply nonexistent.

The transcendental Ego has significant proximity to Kant's *Bewusstsein überhaupt*, his notion of consciousness *per se*, and Kant's doctrine of the transcendental unity of apperception. Husserl stresses the self-conscious subjective aspect of that unity far more than does Kant; nonetheless, the recognition of the similarity is fruitful for understanding Husserl's position. The transcendental Ego is mostly passive, as is Kant's transcendental unity of apperception. Both emphasize the spectatorial and unifying or synthesizing characteristics of the Ego. One would expect to find the passive trait emphasized, since the context in which it occurs is epistemological. Only when the context is ethical could one expect the active, free, spontaneous, and autonomous character of the transcendental Ego or the transcendental unity of apperception to emerge. Both Kant and Husserl find evidence for the existence of this transcendental, unified, and unifying observer in the synthesizing unity which is brought about in and through intentionality.

According to Husserl, the recognition of the existence of transcendental subjectivity or of the transcendental Ego behind all of being is "the greatest of all discoveries" (p. 9). Essentially, that discovery has been the important insight of idealism. Earlier in this introductory essay the remark was made — under the name of "the paradox of definition" — that philosophy in general, and especially phenomenology, presupposes that certain terms have "natural" referents, referents which must be analyzed without the luxury of additional and clarifying definitions. The paradox of definition applies in particular to the analysis and discovery of the transcendental Ego. To understand Husserl we must grant that there is in experience a unique element which can be described, roughly, as the I-pole or transcendental Ego. More specific evidence for the existence and nature of the transcendental Ego is found in the fact that the careful scrutiny of the given in the experience of objects discloses one pervasive and central truth: every object is given or presented to us as an object-for-a-subject. In all experience, the *terminus a quo* is given with precisely the same evidence as the *terminus ad quem*. The Ego is no more a mysterious, inferred, noumenal, or postulated entity than is the object whose essence discloses itself immediately in experience. The ultimate subject is given with the same certitude and immediacy as is any object. This bipolar analysis is as true of the experience of simple physical objects, such as flowers, as of subtle introspective objects, such as personal feelings. The transcendental Ego, furthermore, is not given as an object, but as the subject for which the object manifests itself. Consequently, the Ego is not a thing or a residue of experience, but a ubiquitous single center or pole from which emanate the "radiations" of consciousness and intentionality. Concepts that apply to the world as a whole, to transcendental consciousness or the transcendental realm, are termed "transcendent" by Husserl; whereas whatever applies to the pure Ego, he calls "transcendental." Kant distinguished between both terms, but for him they have different meanings: "transcendent" applies to the noumenal world, and "transcendental" to the phenomenal one.

Once a preliminary insight about the transcendental Ego has been obtained, the strange and paradoxical language used to designate the properties and relations of that Ego becomes more exoteric. In one sense, the transcendental Ego is outside of the world. The Ego is certainly not one item, *i.e.*, object or event, within the world. Sartre rejects the existence of the transcendental Ego on precisely these grounds. In another sense, however, the Ego is the world. As stated earlier, Husserl does not clearly distinguish between the transcendental subject and transcendental consciousness or realm. To the extent that the Ego is the pure stream of consciousness, it is indeed quite proper to say that the Ego is the world. The world of objects is intermeshed with the ever-present matrix of pure consciousness. On the other hand, the Ego cannot be construed to be part of the world, because, as the pure stream of consciousness, the Ego is not one object among others. Also, the transcendental Ego conceived as the perennial observer of existence can quite properly be said to be external to the world, just as the reader is external to the book and the audience is external to the play. The Ego is, instead, an abstraction from the totality of being. The Ego is, in fact, a category — *the* category — of being.

An important and instructive characteristic of the Ego is that attempts at focusing upon it are, a priori, destined to failure because intentionality is a transitive and vectorial, not a reflexive and circular relation, and also because of what may be called the "paradox of self-reference." In the realm of logic a similar problem is discussed under the theory of types. The inquiry into the existence and nature of the ultimate Ego leads to a comparable infinite regress. First, the Ego looks upon an object; then, it retreats, through the epoche, to examine its prior act of vision. It retreats again, through another epoche, and describes this latter examination of the act of vision. This process can continue *ad infinitum*. Or again, the Ego investigates itself as an object; the object thus disclosed is not the transcendental Ego but the empirical ego. The trancendental Ego then focuses on the ego which is investigating that empirical ego. But that third-order ego can in turn be examined. The examiner itself, the observer proper, the *unbeteiligte Zuschauer* (disengaged observer) is mercurial and elusive: it is the camera-eye that focuses, but can never film itself.

The philosophy of language has made a similar discovery. But the philosophy of ordinary-language analysis attributes the difficulty not to an important fact of experience and being, but to a peculiarity of the function and grammar of language. According to Ryle, for example, a proposition refers to a fact, but that fact is extraneous to the proposition itself; that is, the fact cannot be the proposition itself (as Tarski has pointed out, self-reference leads to contradiction [1]). If I wish to refer to the proposition in question, I avail myself of a higher-level proposition, a proposition in a meta-language, and so on, forever. Husserl, however, who operates within the tradition of the analysis of experience rather than of language, views the paradox of self-reference not in terms of a theory of types or meta-languages, but as a unique and important empirically discovered ontological fact.

It is now necessary to explore the philosophic consequences of the paradox of self-reference when applied to the transcendental Ego. Since one of the assumptions in understanding Husserl is that experience has priority over language, the paradoxes on the level of language must be interpreted to be mere reflections of the deeper ontological paradox that is part of the essence of subjectivity. If we abstract carefully, we will discover that the essence of self-referential subjectivity lies in the *pure intentional look* that is perhaps the single most important, and also most apparent, empirically discovered trait of the Ego. The essence of the Ego is disclosed to be this intentional look, the pure intentional vector. Intentionality is thus the invariable structure of the Ego. The intentional look can also be described as the perennial quest for transcendence. The objects of the look are multitudinous; the look itself — like a rainbow over a rushing waterfall — remains steadily the same. From these analyses we can also conclude that the Ego is not part of the world, if by "world" we mean "objectivity." We may assume that language is developed to handle objectivity, so that the transcendental Ego cannot be a referent of ordinary language. Herein lies much of the difficulty of Husserl's exposition of the transcendental Ego.

The Ego is lonely. Notwithstanding his rejection of solipsism, Husserl confesses, in his *Krisis der Europäischen Wissenschaften*, that the transcendental Ego, which he is, is unremittingly lonesome.

The transcendental Ego is, of course, not a premise in the Cartesian sense, that is, for a metaphysical system, since, as Husserl writes, "all arguments ... exist already in transcen-

---

[1] Alfred Tarski, "The Semantic Conception of Truth" (*Philosophy and Phenomenological Research*, Vol. IV, 1944).

dental subjectivity itself" (p. 11). Every conceivable shred of evidence and all confirming experience exist in this prior structure of the transcendental Ego. Consequently, since the Ego is the source of all intentionality and constitution, Husserl feels justified in saying that the transcendental Ego is the source and basis of all knowledge. This Ego constitutes objectivity, proof, language, in fact, everything possible. It follows that the tools which are the creation of the Ego cannot, in turn, be applied to the attempt to understand and measure the Ego itself.

There is another grave problem in connection with Husserl's transcendental reduction, which eventuates in transcendental subjectivity or the transcendental Ego. The transcendental Ego is said to synthesize, construct, and constitute the world. Yet this constitution is preeminently passive and involuntary, a fact which Husserl acknowledges. If we agree, with such phenomenologists as Sartre,[1] that the nature of experiencing or perceiving in man is best described by words such as "freedom" and "spontaneity," then there appears an inherent paradox and contradiction among these propositions: (1) The transcendental Ego is the ultimate constituter of the world; (2) I am, at bottom, the (or a) transcendental Ego; and (3) one of the hallmarks for my being as a conscious being is that I am free and can spontaneously bring about certain states of affairs; I am, in other words, an agent. It follows that the *involuntary* character of *my* constitution of the world is, in turn, freely and deliberately constituted, although the matter has been — also freely — repressed into the unconscious. This situation is either a profound insight into the ultimate structure of being — in which case Husserl's phenomenology, as pointed out before, has strong overtones of objective or absolute idealism, mysticism, and the notions of Atman in Vedanta and Purusha in Sankhya —, or it leads to a *reductio ad absurdum*. Thomas Paine has put it this way,

The sublime and the ridiculous are often so nearly related, that it is difficult to class them separately. One step above the sublime makes the ridiculous, and one step above the ridiculous makes the sublime again.[2]

---

[1] Whether or not one agrees or disagrees with Sartre's general philosophic position, one cannot gainsay the view that his description of the experience of freedom in man is extraordinarily trenchant and cannot be ignored by subsequent philosophies.

[2] *Age of Reason*, Part II, Note.

Husserl did distinguish clearly enough between active and passive constitution, but the notion of passive constitution is paradoxical and perhaps even contradictory, especially in view of the phenomenological basic rule to be true to the appearance of the phenomena themselves. What manifests itself as passive cannot be readily interpreted to be "really" active. To constitute or synthesize means that the ego acts in manipulating the pure refractory or "hyletic" (as Husserl calls these) data. Passive constitution, if such a thing could be, would be *passive acts*, which is a *contradictio in adjecto*.

The technique which eventually leads to the disclosure of the transcendental Ego is the theory of reductions. The transcendental reduction is an analysis of experience that has a great deal in common with the logico-linguistic quest for primitive terms, rules of definition, axioms, rules of procedure, theorems, and criteria of meaningfulness. The basic difference is that the former concentrates on the analysis of experience, whereas the latter is dedicated to the examination of language. These investigations in modern logic are the language-oriented equivalent of Kant's and then Husserl's trancendental methods. Kant's method is the quest for what is necessarily presupposed to make certain experiences in particular, or experience in general, possible. Similarly, the contemporary logical analysis of language seeks to lay bare all the assumptions and disclose all the entailments of linguistic expressions or logical formulae. Finally, for Husserl, the reductions disclose — on the level of experience, not language and logic — the bare and basic elements of pure consciousness. The method of the reductions seeks to uncover all presuppositions which must exist before the kind of experience that we have is possible. For logical and semantical analysis, "presupposition" means specific formal properties of language and of symbols; however, for the experience-oriented transcendental reductions, "presupposition" means necessary, concrete, and underlying structures found in and through the analysis of experience.

"Reduction" derives from the Latin compound *"re-ducere,"* which means "to lead back to origins." A reduction in Husserl's sense is the philosophical effort to circumvent all interpretations, presuppositions, and adventitious aspects of the phenomena themselves. Only by going back to the original and unadulterated presentations of the experiential phenomena themselves can the *facts* of being be adequately understood. To "reduce," therefore, is to exclude, bracket, or leave out of consideration those aspects of our experience of the world which are extraneous to the pure presented phenomena proper.

The reductions, by successively bracketing more and more of the world, and thus leading to a very high level of abstraction, bring out what is necessarily presupposed for the existence and nature of the world as we find it. We can discover the essence of consciousness by placing all that which is not pure consciousness, all that which is contingent to it, in parentheses. This procedure requires a refinement of the epoche. The reductions explore in detail what is left for presentation after the epoche has eliminated or suspended all gratuitous constructions, inferences, and assumptions, principally those dealing with the existence and reality of the external world.

The reductions are partially the anomalous attempt to *invert* the "inevitable" intentional vectorial "look" that underlies all experience. The reductions involve a gradual but systematic and irrevocable "stepping back" from the world, without "looking back." It is as if we notice in the night a sudden beam of blinding light coming from behind us. We are afraid to turn; instead, we step back, gradually, cautiously, but persistently, hoping in this way to discover the source — without ever turning around and looking directly into the painful glare.

The reductions are the outcome of the paradox of self-reference to which examinations of the Ego are susceptible. The reductions represent an effort to circumvent the vectorial *ego-cogito-cogitatum* structure of intentionality. There are many levels, stages, and facets to this retreat.

Certain unique difficulties attend an exposition of Husserl's theory of reductions: The theory grows through many of his works; it is found at many different levels of development; often, while discussing the theory of reductions, Husserl is yet not explicit about the fact that he is dealing with it; finally, his accounts of reduction are sometimes inconsistent and even contradictory. A number of possible interpretations of the reductions are needed to develop and amplify this theory.

Of the phenomena given in experience, there are many and various aspects that can be bracketed. As a rule, a reduction derives its name from the particular element of experience that is bracketed. Throughout his writings, Husserl has bracketed at one time or another the following philosophically important aspects of our experience of the world, with correlatively ensuing special reductions:

(1) We can bracket philosophical theories implicitly presupposed in our apperception of the world. Thus, the *philosophical reduction* is the arduous and detailed effort to detach philosophical theories which may be hidden and implicit in our perception or conception of data.

(2) We can bracket the scientific outlook which is tacitly understood in many of our quotidian experiences as well as in our scientific perceptions. This bracketing may be called the *scientific reduction*. Its employment leads, in Husserl's *Die Krise der europäischen Wissenschaften*, among other results, to his highly heuristic conception of *Lebenswelt*.

(3) We can bracket the belief in the existence of the objective phenomenon under consideration. In this manner we achieve the *phenomenological reduction* or *phenomenological epoche* discussed in Section *a*. This reduction has been developed in far greater detail than any of the others. Also, this reduction leads to important refinements and variations consequent to the suspension of a belief in the existence of the objects under scrutiny. These consequences are embodied in the eidetic and the transcendental reductions.

By abstracting from all possible contingencies, the phenomenological epoche reaches the ultimate, simplest, and absolutely general character of all experience whatever. That character is the intentional stream of consciousness, with its fundamental and pervasive triadic structure as indicated by the formula "*ego cogito cogitata*." To isolate the ego itself is a function relegated to the transcendental reduction.

(4) The *eidetic reduction* focuses and abstracts the general properties, ideas, or forms of the phenomenon under investigation, rather than investigating the differentiating and particularizing elements of the object in question. The eidetic reduction has its prime application, although by no means its only one, in

the study of logic. This reduction illuminates and helps to partially justify Platonic realism, although, again, there exist significant differences between the *eidos* in Husserl and in Plato.

(5) When we bracket literally *everything*, that is, the transcendental reality, all that remains is the pure Ego. This operation is the *transcendental reduction*. In a parallel to Descartes' argument, which Husserl could have drawn but did not draw, we can say that the Ego must exist or be a center of being at least so that it can perform the operation of total bracketing. "Universal bracketing" entails the presence in experience of a pervasive pole which, although pervasive, is not susceptible to focusing or bracketing. Descartes writes, in effect, that even were he perennially deceived by an Almighty Deceiver, he must exist in order to be deceived. Similarly, there must be an Ego in order to bracket everything. Even if the object of consciousness is "nothing at all," there must still be an Ego to make possible the apprehension of that total nothingness. The difference between Husserl and Descartes is primarily that the transcendental reduction enables us to examine the structure of experience, whereas Descartes' *cogito, ergo sum* is more of the order of a deductive inference leading to a certain metaphysical conception. The transcendental reduction leads to the transcendental Ego, a concept discussed earlier in this section.

The reductions can also be presented in terms of the *ego-cogito-cogitatum* triad. Once the existence and reality of the world have been left out of consideration, we can focus on the pure *cogitata*. We can examine the structure of objectivity itself. This activity may be termed also the *eidetic reduction*. Stepping back further, we can analyze the structure of the *cogito*, the act of apprehension or perception. The detached disclosure of the structure of the *cogito* in the total intentional event may be referred to as the *perceptual reduction*, since Husserl does not seem to give it a specific name. Finally, as we approach the genuine source of subjectivity, we get a cluster of reductions.

In that cluster, Husserl begins with another *phenomenological reduction*. This may be interpreted as the initial effort to come to grips with the subject, the I-pole, of all intentional acts. In the process of trying to disclose the Ego in experience, we must objectify that Ego. The analysis of that objectified ego, having successively bracketed all that has come before, is another reduction, which, for lack of a name, we might call the *egological reduction*. We must now step even back of the results of this last reduction. The Ego which effects the egological reduction must be apprehended in turn. This last apprehension, the "encounter" with the true subject, with the original observer of all experience, is called by Husserl the *transcendental reduction*. It is called that because the subject disclosed is the transcendental Ego. The form of apprehension here is altogether atypical, since it does not conform to the *ego-cogito-cogitatum* structure of intentionality. It is here that Husserl introduces the notion of constitution that was discussed earlier.

Finally, in analyzing the structure of the pure transcendental Ego, Husserl discovers that its essence is temporality. This insight is related to Heidegger's well-known emphasis of time in *Sein und Zeit* (*Being and Time*). As a matter of fact, Heidegger edited Husserl's so-called Göttingen lectures on the inner sense of time. The subject constitutes itself, and the matrix within which the transcendental Ego develops or constitutes itself is pure temporality. Again, since Husserl has no name for this reduction, we might appropriately term it the *temporal reduction*. It appears that Husserl comes to agree with Bergson about the centrality of *durée* in the being of the world.

The philosophical importance of the transcendental Ego and the theory of reductions is as important as it is obscure. The basic outlines of Husserl's position are not difficult to envisage; the detailed approach to the various structures and his methodological devices are often rich and always of extraordinary difficulty. Sometimes his analyses seem labored, a bit procrustean, and contrived. However, that his work will have much influence on this and subsequent centuries is hard to question.

(*d*) *Intersubjectivity and the Transcendental Realm*. Because of his tendency towards idealism and concern with the transcendental Ego, Husserl constantly faces the threat of solipsism. His analysis of intersubjectivity and of the transcendental realm are two fundamental efforts to escape that dilemma.

Once the distinction and the interrelation between the transcendental and the empirical ego have been established, solipsism becomes the identification of the entire universe, *i.e.*, the transcendental realm, with the empirical ego. No one takes this absurd position, and Hocking's statement that solipsism or subjective idealism is utterly absurd and utterly irrefutable is false in the present context. On the other hand, the identification of the transcendental realm with the transcendental Ego presents no particular epistemological difficulty, since the transcendental Ego is pure consciousness, one of whose *objects* is the person that I am. The only possible meaning of "otherness" or "externality" is that which arises in the presentations of experience. Linguistic analysis handles this problem by pointing out the contradictory or atypical use of language involved in the epistemological problem of the existence of the external world. Husserl does the same, but he does it from his experience-oriented methodology. The term "externality" refers to one aspect of my *experience*; specifically, it refers to my experience of objects. The study of objectivity can be undertaken only through the careful phenomenological description and analysis of what in pure experience is given as objective. This task is accomplished by the eidetic reduction. The prototype of objectivity is the transcendental realm, that which has earlier been called "transcendental consciousness."

The presence of other persons is a very important type of objectivity or otherness. When Husserl applies the eidetic reduction to other persons, or, in other words, when he brackets through the phenomenological epoche that which makes these particular objects or cogitata *objective*, then he is engaged in what he calls the analysis of the *alter ego* or of transcendental intersubjectivity. The problem of the existence of other minds has meaning and makes sense only on the level of experience or phenomena: there is no other level. Consequently, the study of the nature of other minds consists in isolating the particular kind of objectivity that these have, and analyzing how that objectivity relates itself to the rest of the *Lebenswelt*.

Husserl spent much time and effort analyzing intersubjectivity. Some of the results which he discusses in the *Pariser Vorträge* might be mentioned. There are four aspects of other persons, as these are given to me in experience. Incidentally, it must be remembered that his analysis of other minds purports to be a thoroughly empirical, and thus "scientific" enterprise. (1) Other minds are given to me with and within the experience of "space." But "space" must be interpreted in a wide and psychological sense. The space which other minds occupy is a kind of experienced space; it is not the mathematical and physical space, that is, the dimensional space, with which the physical sciences deal. (2) My experience of other minds discloses them as being interlaced with nature. When I analyze, through the phenomenological reduction, my confrontation, experience, and presentation of another person, I find it impossible to trace a dividing line between the person — in the full and rich meaning of that term — and nature that "surrounds" him. (3) A third factor that enters my experience of other minds is that these appear to me as experiencing the same world that I experience. It follows that empirical investigations of experience disclose solipsism to be a doctrine that is contrary to the facts of experience. If we adopt the phenomenological method, with its reductions, as the final and presuppositionless philosophical method, then we must grant that solipsism is untenable and fantastic. (4) Other persons appear to me as entities that experience me in turn. I consequently do not experience the world as my own private and subjective world, "but as an intersubjective one."

On a more sophisticated level, Husserl recognizes that we experience "access" to other minds through empathy. The transcendental realm, now enriched through the full-bodied incorporation of the *alter ego*, is called by Husserl *"intersubjectively transcendental community"* (p. 35).

The *alter ego*, as is true of all objects, is constituted within the transcendental realm by the transcendental Ego. However, there is a profound difference between the constitution of nature and the constitution of the *alter ego*. Their distinction is to be found in the fact that empathy is part of the intentionality of the *alter ego*. The experienced intimacy between me and the *alter ego*, in other words, the reduction of psychological space through empathy, is a central feature of the manner in which other minds appear to me. Natural objects are impervious to empathy; they are opaque to the unique intentional look that characterizes interpersonal or intersubjective relationships.

(e) *The Logic and the Doctrine of Essences.* In the *Pariser*

Vorträge Husserl makes scant reference to his logic. His studies in this field, however, are both perspicacious and suggestive, and occupy a very large portion of his total work. His logical studies center in three works: the *Philosophie der Arithmetik* (*Philosophy of Arithmetic*, 1891), the *Logische Untersuchungen* (two volumes, 1900–1901), and the *Formale und transzendentale Logik* (1929). Since the language-oriented philosophies of positivism and kindred schools are preeminently concerned with logic, a brief presentation of some of the basic elements in Husserl's logical researches will be of service in further bringing his work to the attention of the English-speaking philosophic world.

Husserl studied under Karl Weierstrass and received his Ph.D. in mathematics. Under the influence of Brentano, Husserl tried to develop psychologism, the view that logic is a species of psychology, but then, partially due to Gottlob Frege, gave up this once popular interpretation of mathematics. It is interesting to note and not widely known that both Russell and Husserl knew early of each other's work. Husserl thought Russell's logical researches too far removed from concrete reality and experience to be of genuine value to the foundations of logic and mathematics. Russell, however, held Husserl's *Logische Untersuchungen* in high esteem.[1]

Husserl's logic is in part an extension and elaboration of scholastic and realistic philosophy. His conception of logic is in general the view that logic is the science of a specific class of "objects." These objects are said to exist in the world and in our experience; they are given to us in immediate apprehension. These objects are properly called "essences." In this way logic becomes an "empirical" or experiential study of essences (*Wesenswissenschaft*); logic is thus an "eidetic science" which avails itself of the intuition of essences (*Wesensschau*). Logic is consequently a concrete, experiential, and ontological study. That is, logical structures — including logical or apodictic necessity — are empirically discernible aspects of our experience of essences or logical objects. In contradistinction to the theory supporting contemporary logic, where logic is symbolic, arbitrary, and decisional, for Husserl, logic, as all else, is enmeshed in experience,

---

[1] *Cf.* Herbert Spiegelberg, *op. cit.*, p. 93, n. 1.

and is studied by the proper abstraction from experience. Logical investigation thus becomes the exploration of certain general, important, and clearly specifiable traits of experience. Husserl is careful to avoid the naive empiricism in logic that he alleges is found in Eighteenth and Ninetheenth century British philosophers; in other words, he rejects their "psychologism." In the process of so doing he anticipates many developments in positivism, linguistic analysis, and symbolic logic. Philosophical analysis and phenomenology share important insights regarding the nature and function of logic, meaning, and language. Their terminology, of course, differs, so that the similarities are not immediately apparent; but had Husserl's *Logische Untersuchungen* been published in English translation at an early date, rather than his *Ideen*, his influence today on the English-speaking world would be far more substantial than in fact it is. We must remember that the *Logische Untersuchungen* were published at the turn of the century, long before the appearance of the main works of Russell, Wittgenstein, and the Vienna Circle.

However, notwithstanding important similarities, one must never loose sight of the basic difference between analytic philosophy and phenomenology. Phenomenology, when applied to logic, proceeds through an analysis of essences and their relations as these present themselves to our experience; and here the term "experience" is used in the wide sense of idealistic philosophies. Kant's analysis of mathematics, for example, makes good sense when interpreted to be the phenomenological description of our sense of certainty, and the investigation of the structure and manner of presentation of the objects or entities that are of concern to mathematics, such as cardinal number, set, addition, probability, and the like. The analytic school, on the other hand, rejects Kant's theories. Russell's criticism of Kant in the former's *Principles of Mathematics* [1], that Kant's intuitional conception of mathematics is in error because all mathematics can be formally deduced from pure logic, is possible only in the light of a non-phenomenological, non-empirical, non-realistic, and non-ontological interpretation (hence, misinterpretation) of Kant's epistemology, whereas for phenomenology, Kant's intuitive ap-

---

[1] Bertrand Russell, *Principles of Mathematics*, 2nd ed. (New York: W. W. Norton, 1937), p. 4.

proach to mathematics is correct in its general outlines although perhaps wanting somewhat in its detailed exposition.

The present discussion is divided into four parts: their subjects are the acts and objects in logic, the levels of logic, the ontological status of logical structures, and a brief outline of the *Logische Untersuchungen*, perhaps Husserl's most important work in this area.

(a) The Acts and Objects in Logic. A number of characteristics specify the nature of logical investigation, and set off logical objects from objects of other types. The investigation is *intuitive* and the objects are such that they lend themselves to intuitive analysis. The analyses of the nature of logical structures that one finally accepts are self-evident, axiomatic; no reasons or evidence — in the deductive, inductive, or discursive sense — can be given for the validity of arguments, rules of procedure, definitions, and postulates. The subject-matter of logic is, after all, the investigation of the pure and immediate data of the experience or conscious presentation of logical truths. The investigation is also *descriptive*. Logical objects can be experienced and described. The phenomenological analysis of logical structures is the description of our confrontation, in conscious experience, with logical relations and certitudes. The objects and the nature of the investigation are *non-sensory*. That is to say, logical and mathematical objects and relations are indeed part of experience; but the type of experience that gives us these truths is not of the ordinary sensory or perceptual character. Furthermore, the investigation and its objects are *a priori*, for the phenomenological investigation of logical objects discloses their necessity and universality. It is thus legitimate to say that necessity and universality are the empirically discovered traits of logical essences as these essences present themselves to us in the unique type of experience in which they are intuited.

Husserl's initial theory of logic was psychologistic. He then emphatically rejected the possibility of reducing logic to psychological states and generalizations thereof. Logical structures are *objects* given in experience. However, if the expression "psychological data" is given a sufficiently broad extension, far greater than is usual, then there can be no fundamental objection to asserting the ulitmate coalescence of psychology and phenomenology, and, consequently, of the close link between psychology and logic.

The objects or essences in logical inquiry are *abstractions*. Specifically, logic and mathematics deal with the highest level of abstractions — somewhat like the classes of classes, in terms of which Russel defines "number." Finally, logical essences are *universals* (*allgemeine Gegenstände*). Husserl rejects the nominalism of the British empiricists, for whom the universal is merely an icon or a fleeting and shifting mental image. Husserl contends that the universal is experienced as an unchanging, eternal meaning or content. Not only does he maintain that universals are objects apprehended in experience; the very acts of consciousness which apprehend these universal essences are altogether different from the acts of consciousness through which we perceive particular objects. This difference in acts is the difference in constitution and intentionality.

(b) Levels of Logic. The first and most general level of logic is the one that treats of the mere possibilities of propositions. This activity was predominantly practiced by the ancient Greeks, who studied the formal properties of propositions as divorced from their instantiations or specific meanings. As this highest level of generality, the Greeks were concerned mainly with the classification of propositions, rather than with questions of validity and inference.

At the second level, which is of slightly greater specificity than the previous one, logical investigation examines the nature of validity and empirical reference, which, for Husserl, are the implications of the principle of non-contradiction. These implications cover the whole range of the relations between propositions, especially immediate and mediate arguments, but in addition also cover the rules of inference, which, for Husserl, are referred to as basic logical "truths." The distinction between these two levels — as Husserl develops it — has some relation with terminological differentiations in modern semiotics. What has come to be called "syntactics" or "syntactical rules," the rules governing the pure relations of symbols, Husserl calls, in effect, *apophantics*. On the other hand, "semantics" or "semantical rules," which are the rules of reference governing the relation of words to things, is handled by what Husserl's calls *formal ontology*.

The third level is a break with the Aristotelian tradition. Here Husserl extends his investigations beyond the pure formal characteristics of logical objects: he examines how logical objects arise within the concrete world. That is, he interprets logical objects as intentions, as essences which are constituted by the transcendental Ego. At this level of his investigations, Husserl is outside both the Aristotelian and positivistic approaches and operates within the experiential tradition of Brentano. In sum, for Husserl, Logic has an objective ontological basis and a subjective genesis.

This third level brings out the doctrine of intentionality. Husserl assumes and then presents evidence for the fact that the intentional act of apprehension is significantly parallel to its objective correlates. The act is characterized as *noetic*, and the objective correlate, as *noematic*. Consequently, in order to understand the objects of logical and mathematical inquiry, we must examine the intentional and constitutive acts — the cogitationes — in addition to the objects themselves. Husserl writes in the *Pariser Vorträge* that the object or *cogitatum* serves as clue to the nature of the particular *cogitationes* or constitutive acts in question. This general principle also applies to logical and mathematical objects.

The separation of the third level from the first two is accentuated by Husserl's terminology. Logic, considered in its pure abstraction, is *formal*; but when the problem of the concrete existence of logical objects and their intentional constitution is analyzed, then one deals with *transcendental* logic.

(c) The Ontological Status of Logical Structures. Husserl can be interpreted to hold that the rules of logic are neither arbitrary, decisional, or stipulative, nor are they normative. Instead, logical laws are a certain class of facts. The rules of logic, then, apply to facts, not propositions. The law of contradiction does not assert that contradictory propositions do not exist, nor that they ought not to exist; it is perfectly possible to formulate contradictory expressions. Contradictory expressions do exist. The law does assert — and with intuitively given apodicticity — that no substance can possess contradictory or mutually exclusive predicates. Husserl thus rejects the purely nominalistic interpretation of logical objects.

On the other hand, if logic were a branch of psychology — rather than a unique phenomenological science — then the properties of logical objects, being laws of mental events, would be vague, changeable, and merely probable. However, none of these attributes characterizes our knowledge of logical objects. Furthermore, if logic were a branch of psychology, then the existence of logical objects, with their properties and relations, would have to presuppose the existence of mental events. This assumption is no problem in idealism, but truths about logical objects are prior to any metaphysical commitments.

Husserl's detailed criticism of "psychologism" or "psychognosticism" appears in the first volume of his *Logische Untersuchungen*. This criticism suggests the later interpretation of logic as analytic found in Russel and the positivists. Both Russell and Husserl maintain that logic and mathematics cannot be grounded on a psychology of thought. As stated before, Husserl did try psychologism once, in his *Philosophie der Arithmetik*, but found the task impossible. He shows quite clearly that logic is not the psychological study of the laws governing thought processes. As a matter of fact, a description of thought processes discloses that people do not think logically most of the time. Logic possesses criteria of truth and validity that are altogether unique, independent, and have no sensory basis.

What remains is the status of meaning itself. "Meaning" has three significations. First of all, it is the term, symbol, sentence, or expression that articulates, points, and communicates. Second, meaning involves a referent. This referent need not be a physical object. In mathematics, the referents are pure essences. The act of reference can be achieved through — using contemporary terminology — either designation or denotation. The distinctions between sentence and proposition as well as between a term and its referent are introduced to account for the fact that many sentences can denote one and the same proposition. Husserl thus distinguishes between the term, expression, or articulation (*Ausdruck*), and its significance, content, meaning, or referent (*Bedeutung*).

Husserl makes distinctions and develops concepts with respect to the nature of language which are a genuine contribution to the linguistic analysis prevalent today. For example, he calls attention to the fact that part of the meaning of a term, expression, or sentence is what it tacitly tells us about the speaker or writer himself. The referential arrow of meaning thus points not only to the object meant but also to the person who "intends" the use of language.

Another important distinction, which follows naturally from the applications of the phenomenological method, is between the word itself and its multifarious, varied, and rich intuitive content. This intuitive mass is more important in expression, understanding, and communication than the so-called dictionary definition of words. Philosophic and other problems that arise in and through language occur principally within this intuitive mass, which is vague and shifts with associations, memories, anticipations, moods, etc.

The further distinction between act and thing (*noesis* and *noema*) becomes necessary and manifest when the intentional act of meaning refers to the null class, or when several and different expressions of acts of meaning refer to one and the same object. The meaning of meaning must not be restricted to the analysis of words, but must be found in an examination of the intentions embodied in them and the objective correlates which may or may not fulfill the anticipations of these intentional acts.

(d) Outline of the *Logische Untersuchungen*. The material previously mentioned, and much more, is worked out, with its detailed ramifications, in Husserl's main work on logic. First, Husserl develops his critique of psychologism. Of the six ensuing studies, the first is titled "Expression and Meaning" (*Ausdruck und Bedeutung*). In it he examines the nature and structure of the acts which bestow meaning on linguistic expressions. In the second section, "The Ideal Unity of the Species and the Newer Theories of Abstractions" (*Die ideale Einheit der Spezies und die neueren Abstraktionstheorien*), Husserl discusses various theories of abstractions found in the British empiricist philosophers. Here he analyzes and contrasts the mode of apprehension that characterizes our experience of universals with our mode of experiencing particular abstractions of individual objects. These latter, particularized, abstractions are called "moments." The crucial difference between the particular and the universal appears in the structure of the conscious and intentional act that focuses on the *cogitatum* in question. This is one of Husserl's central and recurring themes.

The third section concerns the "Doctrine of Wholes and Parts" (*Zur Lehre von den Ganzen und Teilen*) and it discusses the relation of inherence that obtains between the object as a whole and its moments or individual abstractions. The fourth section is "The Distinction between Independent and Dependent Meanings" (*Der Unterschied der selbständigen und unselbständigen Bedeutungen*). Here Husserl discusses the distinction between categorematic and syncategorematic words, not as to their grammatical function, but in terms of their difference in intentional constitution. The fifth study is "About Intentional Experiences and their 'Contents'" (*Über intentionale Erlebnisse und ihre "Inhalte"*). This is a further analysis of the intentional structure of meaning. Husserl separates the act of experiencing, with its directions and qualities, from the content or matter towards which that act is directed.

His last section is a very important epistemological exposition. It deals with the "Elements of a Phenomenological Elucidation of Knowledge" (*Elemente einer phänomenologischen Aufklärung der Erkenntnis*). Some of this material is discussed in the *Pariser Vorträge*. Husserl distinguishes between bestowing and fulfilling meaning, a distinction that, by emphasizing the nexus between meaning and confirmation, coincides with pragmatic and positivistic theories of meaning. Meaning involves prediction and anticipation. This aspect of meaning is the "intention of meaning" (*Bedeutungs-intention*). But meaning also involves confirmation, verification, the fulfillment of anticipation. This second characteristic of the experience of meaning is the "fulfillment of meaning" (*Bedeutungserfüllung*). As has been discussed already, the fundamental difference between Husserl's view and that of pragmatism and especially of positivism is that the term "experience" has a much wider meaning for the former than it does for the naturalistic orientation found in positivism.

5. Husserl's Influence and His Relation to Other Doctrines

This introductory essay is not the place for an extended appraisal of Husserl's influence and relation to other doctrines. The study of this connection is a major topic in contemporary philosophy. Even if space would permit, the task presents its peculiar difficulties, since the importance of Husserl is not likely to be assessed authoritatively and definitively until much later in this century — or later. The present section will therefore be limited to suggest a few areas of influence, relation, and continuing importance.

A number of recent and contemporary philosophers endeavored to continue the work of Husserl directly. Among these, the following stand out: Max Scheler (1874–1928), Alexander Pfänder (1870–1941), Moritz Geiger (1880–1937), Adolph Reinach (1883–1916), Roman Ingarden (b. 1893), Oskar Becker (b. 1889), Edith Stein (1891–1942), Hedwig Conrad-Martius (b. 1888), and Alexander Koyré (b. 1892). In the United States, of particular importance and influence in spreading phenomenology have been Marvin Farber (b. 1910), Fritz Kaufmann (1891–1958), John Wild (b. 1902), Aron Gurwitch (b. 1901), and Alfred Schuetz (1899–1959).

Indirectly phenomenology has been of influence on the ontology of Nicolai Hartmann (1882–1950), the existential ontology of Martin Heidegger (b. 1889), the psychopathology of Karl Jaspers (b. 1883), the psychology of Maurice Merleau-Ponty (1907–1961), and on the general existentialist philosophies of Jean-Paul Sartre (b. 1905) and Gabriel Marcel (b. 1889).

Although the existentialist philosophers often refer to their works as "phenomenologies," there are important differences between Husserl and these putative successors of his. Existentialism has been influenced by Husserl's notion of epoche. This characteristic aspect of the phenomenological technique has been applied to the human situation, to the question of the meaning of life, and to the experience of feeling human or of being in the world. The existentialists tend to ignore the more technical epistemological and metaphysical aspects of Husserl's thought. Among these must be listed the theories of constitution, the reductions leading to the transcendental Ego, the idealistic tendencies and implications, and the view that logic has ontological import. Sartre, for example, is explicit in rejecting the doctrine of the transcendental Ego. Also, through the emphasis on action, he rejects the notion of potentiality, a simulacrum of which emerges in Husserl under the doctrine of horizons. The existentialists ignore Husserl's general system, and restrict their interest to the phenomenological epoche. They prefer the concrete drama of lived experience to the abstract, esoteric, and purely philosophic language of Husserl; consequently, we frequently find existentialist themes expressed in literary forms.

Husserl's relation to idealism is both ambiguous and profound. His philosophical position cannot be understood without clearly perceiving its subjectivistic and idealistic orientations. However, it is being unjust to Husserl and insentive to his philosophical insights to classify him, without further qualifications, as an idealist. The "semantic horizon" of idealism in metaphysics involves entailments and assumptions — such as quantitative metaphysical dualism and the immateriality of mind — that are contrary to Husserl's contentions and equally opposed to the facts of experience. In the *Pariser Vorträge* Husserl refers to his view as a "transcendental idealism," which he says is an idealism in a new sense. This idealism transcends the mind-matter and inner-outer dualisms that must be presupposed before the identification of the universe with mind can be a meaningful and synthetic assertion. Husserl's new idealism criticizes the so-called old idealism in the same way that linguistic analysis does. Husserl says, in effect, that traditional idealism is either tautologous — if mind is construed to be equivalent to the totality of being — or meaningless (or false) — if the totality of being is identified with only part of it, namely mind. However, Husserl does not get out of the very difficult dilemma that is presented by his flirtation with idealism. This dilemma is one of the grave problems facing contemporary phenomenologists. Perhaps the significant discovery that Husserl's idealistic and subjectivistic orientations provide is that, according to the empirical facts of experience, all being is related in some fashion to the ego-pole that I am. This relation, in its most general terms, is characterized by the perception, apprehension, thinking about, or accessibility of being.

Although Husserl opposes many traditional metaphysical

positions, he does not reject metaphysics *per se*. Here his position differs from that of linguistic analysis. He writes that he discards only those aspects of metaphysics which are self-contradictory. As was pointed out several times earlier in this essay, Husserl's quasi-metaphysics is not unlike certain aspects of Oriental philosophy. Whereas the existentialists tend to reject Husserl's metaphysical interests, his concern with the transcendental Ego, and his idealistic orientation, Oriental philosophy is consistent with his insights in these areas. There are, for instance, interesting connections between his theory of reductions and certain meditation exercises in Yoga. A fundamental difference remains, of course, between Husserl's position and Oriental philosophy. It consists in the goal of inquiry, which, for Oriental thought is directed toward religious insights and salvation, but for Husserl is restricted to purely theoretical questions. Research on Husserl today is found, above all, in Catholic centers of learning. This fact is perhaps evidence for the current awareness that Husserl philosophized in the tradition of metaphysics, particularly scholastic and realistic ontology. The connection between Husserl's position and metaphysics is therefore of the first importance.

One of the important tasks for contemporary philosophic scholars is to explore the relations between linguistic analysis and positivism on the one hand, and phenomenology and existentialism on the other. Throughout this introductory essay frequent references to this problem have been made. As was stated, perhaps the most characteristic difference between these approaches is the relative ontological priority ascribed to language and experience, so that for one methodology philosophy is the exploration of experience and for the other it is the exploration of language. The general criticisms of traditional philosophic problems and their common proposed solutions are very much alike in these two philosophical approaches. Husserl adjudges many philosophic problems meaningless on grounds similar to those presented by linguistic analysis. Husserl's exploration of the foundations of logic and mathematics, however, is carried out in a "transcendental" fashion; that is to say, he searches for the essence of logic not in an arbitrary and formal system of symbols, but in the structure of pure consciousness itself.

Existentialism has been influential on psychiatry, psycho-
analysis, and psychology in a movement variously referred to as
existential psychiatry or existential analysis. To the extent that
Husserl is one of the precursors of existentialism, his phenomenological technique has affinities with this new movement in
psychotherapy, which in turn resembles the classical Freudian
theories. Not only did both Freud and Husserl live at approxi-
mately the same time (Freud lived from 1856 to 1939, Husserl
from 1859 to 1938), study under Franz Brentano, and write
important works at the turn of the century (Freud's *Interpretation of Dreams* was published in 1900, and Husserl's *Logical
Investigations* appeared in 1900 and 1901), but above all there are
important affinities between Husserl's phenomenological epoche
and Freud's basic rule (free-association). The process of psychotherapy is a systematic and repeated application of the kind
of honesty and distancing that is characteristic of the epoche.
It can be argued that psychotherapy is the epoche applied to
one's personal life[1].

THE LIFE OF HUSSERL AND THE ARCHIVES AT LOUVAIN

Edmund Husserl was born on April 8, 1859, in Prossnitz, which
is in the Bohemian province of Moravia. Husserl's birth con-
tributes to the philosophic distinction enjoyed by that year. It
was the year of the publication of Darwin's *Origin of Species*,
and of John Stuart Mill's *Essay on Liberty*. It was also the year
in which were born John Dewey, Henri Bergson, and Samuel
Alexander. Husserl was of Jewish origin, but in 1887 he received
a Lutheran baptism. During his student days in Leipzig, Berlin,
and Vienna, he had prolific interests, concentrating on astronomy,
mathematics, physics, psychology, and philosophy. Among his
distinguished teachers one must mention above all Franz Brentano (1838–1917), who turned Husserl to philosophy, and who
was the greatest single influence in the philosophic life of Husserl.
However, Husserl's intellectual separation from Brentano
increased over the years. Husserl studied mathematics under
Karl Weierstrass (1815–1817) and the psychology of his good

---

[1] *Cf.* Peter Koestenbaum, "Phenomenological Foundations for the Behavioral
Sciences," *Journal of Existentialism*, Spring, 1966, 305–341.

friend Carl Stumpf (1848–1936), whose works he read assiduously. He also heard the philosophy lectures of Friedrich Paulsen in Berlin. Husserl's mature thought begins with a concern for the foundations of mathematics, continues with the development of the phenomenological method, and concludes with the kind of idealism that is associated with his doctrine of the transcendental Ego. These three periods of thought correspond roughly to his three teaching positions. He was *Privatdozent* at Halle from 1887–1901, after which he occupied a position at Göttingen up to 1916, leading to full professor. He then moved to a professorship at Freiburg im Breisgau, where he taught from 1916 to 1929. Because of his Judaism, Husserl was stripped of his professorship and teaching privileges by the Nazis in 1933. He was also forbidden to participate in philosophic congresses, even as a private citizen. Thereupon the University of Southern California offered Husserl a professorship, which he declined: he wanted to die where he had spent his life teaching. On April 27, 1938, after an illness of five months, and at the age of 79, Edmund Husserl died.

He left behind 40,000 pages of unpublished manuscripts in stenographic form, 5,000 of which had already been transcribed. He also left a large and valuable library including many first editions. Many of these 4500 books were filled with his own illuminating apostils. The discovery of this immense manuscript library led the Franciscan priest Herman Leo Van Breda to establish the Husserl Archives at Louvain.

The purpose of the Husserl Archives, headed by Dr. Van Breda, and located at the old Brabantic school of Louvain (Leuven) in Belgium, is fourfold. First, its goal is to house the Husserl manuscripts, letters, and books. Second, at Louvain the manuscripts are transcribed and carefully edited. Third, the Archives serve as a center of research on Husserl and phenomenology. Finally, the Archives publish critical editions of the works of Husserl, as well as related scholarly research projects.[1] Copies of transcriptions made at the Archives are available in several

---

[1] The Archives have been responsible for the publication of two distinguished series: *Husserliana* (the collected works of Edmund Husserl) and *Phaenomenologica* (critical, historical, and original work in the area of phenomenology). Both are under the direction of H. L. Van Breda, and are published by Martinus Nijhoff, The Hague, Netherlands.

countries. In the United States these are to be found at the University of Pennsylvania.[1]

The rescue of Husserl's manuscript heritage from the hands of the Nazis occurred at the time of the Munich crisis in 1938 and is an authentic cloak-and-dagger story[2]. The principals displayed redoubtable foresight and dedication. These were not only Van Breda, but also Malvine Husserl, widow of the philosopher, Husserl's two assistants, Ludwig Landgrebe and Eugen Fink — who were among the very few who could transcribe Husserl's shorthand —, and Paul-Henri Spaak, then Prime Minister of Belgium.

After several unsuccessful attempts to sneak the manuscripts across the Swiss border as a nun's baggage or to interest a Belgian consulate to take charge of the bulky materials, Van Breda persuaded the Belgian Embassy in Berlin to declare the suitcases containing the manuscripts as Belgian property and thus have them covered by the immunity of the diplomatic pouch. This declaration required the cooperation of the administrative officials at Louvain, a directive from the Prime Minister of Belgium, and the transfer of ownership of the manuscripts from Malvine Husserl to Van Breda, a Belgian citizen, with a corresponding counter-transfer testifying to the necessarily spurious and *pro tempore* character of that transfer.

Eventually, Malvine Husserl was assisted in escaping to Belgium. Upon the German invasion and occupation of Belgium, from 1939 to 1945, Husserl's widow went into hiding in a convent (she converted to Catholicism in 1941), and the manuscripts, as well as the existence of the Archives themselves, had to be once more protected from the German vandalism against anything Jewish. Almost all manuscripts miraculously survived the war. This was not true of Husserl's correspondence, including letters from Heidegger, an important part of which was destroyed, ironically, during an allied bombing raid on Antwerp.

---

[1] *Cf.* Herman Leo Van Breda, "Geist und Bedeutung des Husserl-Archivs," in *Edmund Husserl, 1859–1959* (The Hague: Martinus Nijhoff, 1959) pp. 116–122.

[2] See the interesting and detailed account in H. L. Van Breda, "Le sauvetage de l'héritage husserlien et la fondation des Archives-Husserl" in *Husserl et la Pensée Moderne* (The Hague: Martinus Nijhoff, 1959) pp. 1–42.

The *Pariser Vorträge* are a pair of two-hour papers delivered, in German, on February 23 and 25, 1929, at the Sorbonne, under the title "Introduction to Transcendental Phenomenology." The occasion was an accolade to Husserl, sponsored by the *Académie Française*. Present, among distinguished scholars, was the German ambassador. These lectures, with modifications, were later repeated in Strasbourg, and eventually expanded into the *Cartesianische Meditationen*. The *Pariser Vorträge* thus represent an introduction into the mature thought of Edmund Husserl and in the author's own words. The text on which the present translation is based is found in Volume I of *Husserliana*, and is Dr. Strasser's reconstruction of the original.

Dr. Strasser has made an extensive, scholarly, and commendable effort to rebuild the original text of these lectures from the oldest sketches and versions of the *Cartesianische Meditationen*. He has tried to cull the original wording from its later development in the published *Cartesianische Meditationen*. The result of his research is published in *Husserliana I*. On pages 225–233 of that work, Dr. Strasser lists all marginal and other notes found in the originals at the Husserl Archives. The following translation does not include the marginal notations and changes referred to in Dr. Strasser's critical comments.

THE PARIS LECTURES

I am filled with joy at the opportunity to talk about the new 〈3〉
phenomenology at this most venerable place of French learning,
and for very special reasons. No philosopher of the past has
affected the sense of phenomenology as decisively as René
Descartes, France's greatest thinker. Phenomenology must honor
him as its genuine patriarch. It must be said explicitly that the
study of Descartes' *Meditations* has influenced directly the formation of the developing phenomenology and given it its
present form, to such an extent that phenomenology might
almost be called a new, a twentieth century, Cartesianism.

Under these circumstances I may have advance assurance
of your interest, especially if I start with those themes in the
Meditationes de prima philosophia which are timeless, and if
through them I point out the transformations and new concepts
which give birth to what is characteristic of the phenomenological
method and its problems.

Every beginner in philosophy is familiar with the remarkable
train of thought in the *Meditations*. Their goal, as we remember,
is a complete reform of philosophy, including all the sciences,
since the latter are merely dependent members of the one universal body of knowledge which is philosophy. Only through
systematic unity can the sciences achieve genuine rationality,
which, as they have developed so far, is missing. What is needed
is a radical reconstruction which will *satisfy* the ideal of philosophy as being the *universal unity of knowledge* by means of a
unitary and *absolutely rational foundation*. Descartes carries out
the demand for reconstruction in terms of a subjectively oriented
philosophy. This subjective turn is carried out in two steps./

First, anyone who seriously considers becoming a philosopher 〈4〉
must once in his life withdraw into himself and then, from within

attempt to destroy and rebuild all previous learning. Philosophy is the supremely personal affair of the one who philosophizes. It is the question of *his sapientia universalis*, the aspiration of *his* knowledge for the universal. In particular, the philosopher's quest is for truly scientific knowledge, knowledge for which he can assume — from the very beginning and in every subsequent step — complete responsibility by using *his* own absolutely self-evident justifications. I can become a genuine philosopher only by freely choosing to focus my life on this goal. Once I am thus committed and have accordingly chosen to begin with total poverty and destruction, my first problem is to discover an absolutely secure starting point and rules of procedure, when, in actual fact, I lack any support from the existing disciplines. Consequently, the Cartesian meditations must not be viewed as the private affair of the philosopher Descartes, but as the necessary prototype for the meditations of any beginning philosopher whatsoever.

When we now turn our attention to the content of the *Meditations*, a content which appears rather strange to us today, we notice immediately a *return to the philosophizing ego* in a second and deeper sense. It is the familiar and epoch-making return to the ego as subject of his pure *cogitationes*. It is the ego which, while it suspends all beliefs about the reality of the world on the grounds that these are not indubitable, discovers itself as the only apodictically certain being.

The ego is engaged, first of all, in philosophizing that is seriously solipsistic. He looks for apodictically certain and yet purely subjective procedures through which an objective external world can be deduced. Descartes does this in a well-known manner. He first infers both the existence and *veracitas* of God. Then, through their mediation, he deduces objective reality as a dualism of substances. In this way he reaches the objective ground of knowledge and the particular sciences themselves as well. All his inferences are based on immanent principles, *i.e.*, principles which are innate to the ego.

So much for Descartes. We now ask, is it really worthwhile to hunt critically for the eternal significance of these thoughts?/
⟨5⟩ Can these infuse life into our age?

Doubt is raised, in any event, by the fact that the positive sciences, for which the meditations were to have served as absolutely rational foundation, have paid so very little attention to them. Nonetheless, and despite the brilliant development experienced by the sciences over the last three centuries, they feel themselves today seriously limited by the obscurity of their foundations. But it scarcely occurs to them to refer to the Cartesian meditations for the reformulation of their foundations.

On the other hand, serious consideration must be given to the fact that the meditations constitute an altogether unique and epochal event in the history of philosophy, specifically because of their return to the *ego cogito*. As a matter of fact, Descartes inaugurates a completely new type of philosophy. Philosophy, with its style now changed altogether, experiences a radical conversion from naive objectivism to *transcendental subjectivism*. This subjectivism strives toward a pure end-form through efforts that are constantly renewed yet always remain unsatisfactory. Might it not be that this continuing tendency has eternal significance? Perhaps it is a vast task assigned to us by history itself, invoking our collective cooperation.

The splintering of contemporary philosophy and its aimless activity make us pause. Must this situation not be traced back to the fact that the motivations from which Descartes' meditations emanate have lost their original vitality? Is it not true that the only fruitful renaissance is one which reawakens these meditations, not in order to accept them, but to reveal the profound truth in the radicalism of a return to the *ego cogito* with the eternal values that reside therein?

In any case, this is the path that led to transcendental phenomenology.

Let us now pursue this path together. In true Cartesian fashion, we will become philosophers meditating in a radical sense, with, of course, frequent and critical modifications of the older Cartesian meditations. What was merely germinal in them must be freely developed here.

We thus begin, everyone for himself and in himself, with the de/cision to disregard all our present knowledge. We do not give ⟨6⟩ up Descartes' guiding goal of an absolute foundation for knowledge. At the beginning, however, to presuppose even the possibility of that goal would be prejudice. We are satisfied to discover

the goal and nature of science by submerging ourselves in
scientific activity. It is the spirit of science to count nothing as
really scientific which cannot be fully justified by the evidence.
In other words, science demands proof *by reference to the things
and facts themselves, as these are given in actual experience and
intuition.* Thus guided, we, the beginning philosophers, make it a
rule to judge only by the evidence. Also, the evidence itself must
be subjected to critical verification, and that on the basis, of
course, of further available evidence. Since from the beginning
we have disregarded the sciences, we operate within our pre-
scientific life, which is likewise filled with immediate and mediate
evidences. This, and nothing else, is first given to us.

Herein arises our first question. Can we find evidence that
is both immediate and apodictic? Can we find evidence that is
primitive, in the sense that it must by necessity precede all
other evidence?

As we meditate on this question one thing does, in fact, emerge
as both prior to all evidence and as apodictic. It is the existence
of the world. All science refers to the world, and, before that, our
ordinary life already makes reference to it. *That the being of the
world precedes everything is* so *obvious* that no one thinks to
articulate it in a sentence. Our experience of the world is continuous, incessant, and unquestionable. But is it true that this
experiential evidence, even though taken for granted, is really
apodictic and primary to all other evidence? We will have to
deny both. Is it not the case that occasionally something manifests itself as a sensory illusion? Has not the coherent and unified
totality of our experience been at times debased as a mere
dream? We will ignore Descartes' attempt to prove that, notwithstanding the fact of its being constantly experienced, the
⟨7⟩ world's nonbeing can be conceived. / His proof is carried out by a
much too superficial criticism of sensory experience. We will
keep this much: experiential evidence that is to serve as radical
foundation for knowledge needs, above all, a critique of its
validity and range. It cannot be accepted as apodictic without
question and qualification. Therefore, merely to disregard all
knowledge and to treat the sciences as prejudices is not enough.
Even the experience of the world as the true universal ground of
knowledge becomes an unacceptably naive belief. We can no

longer accept the reality of the world as a fact to be taken for granted. *It is a hypothesis that needs verification.*

Does there remain a ground of being? Do we still have a basis for all judgments and evidences, a basis on which a universal philosophy can rest apodictically? Is not "world" the name for the totality of all that is? Might it not turn out that the world is not the truly ultimate basis for judgment, but instead that its existence presupposes a prior ground of being?

Here, specifically following Descartes, we make the great shift which, when properly carried out, leads to *transcendental subjectivity*. This is the shift to the *ego cogito*, as the apodictically certain and *last basis for judgment* upon which all radical philosophy must be grounded.

Let us consider: as radically meditating philosophers we now have neither knowledge that is valid for us nor a world that exists for us. We can no longer say that the world is real — a belief that is natural enough in our ordinary experience —; instead, it merely makes a claim to reality. This skepticism also applies to other selves, so that we rightly should not speak communicatively, that is, in the plural. Other people and animals are, of course, given to me only through sensory experience. Sine I have questioned the validity of the latter I cannot avail myself of it here. With the loss of other minds I lose, of course, all forms of sociability and culture. In short, the entire concrete world ceases to have reality for me and becomes instead mere appearance. However, whatever may be the veracity of the claim to being made by phenomena, whether they represent reality or appearance, phenomena in themselves / cannot be disregarded as mere "nothing." On the contrary, it is ⟨8⟩ precisely the phenomena themselves which, without exception, render possible for me the very existence of both reality and appearance. Again, I may freely abstain from entertaining any belief about experience — which I did. This simply means that I refuse to assert the reality of the world. Nonetheless, we must be careful to realize that this epistemological abstention is still what it is: it includes the whole stream of experienced life and all its particulars, the appearances of objects, other people, cultural situations, etc. Nothing changes, except that I no longer accept the world simply as real; I no longer judge regarding the distinction between reality and appearance. I must similarly abstain from any other of my opinions, judgments, and valuations about the world, since these likewise assume the reality of the world. But for these, as for other phenomena, epistemological abstention does not mean their disappearance, at least not as pure phenomena.

This ubiquitous detachment from any point of view regarding the objective world we term the *phenomenological epoché*. It is the methodology through which I come to understand myself as that ego and life of consciousness in which and through which the entire objective world exists for me, and is for me precisely as it is. Everything in the world, all spatio-temporal being, exists for me because I experience it, because I perceive it, remember it, think of it in any way, judge it, value it, desire it, etc. It is well known that Descartes designates all this by the term *cogito*. For me the world is nothing other than what I am aware of and what appears valid in such *cogitationes*. *The whole meaning and reality of the world rests exclusively on such cogitationes*. My entire worldly life takes its course within these. I cannot live, experience, think, value, and act in any world which is not in some sense in me, and derives its meaning and truth from me. If I place myself above that entire life and if I abstain from any commitment about reality, specifically one which accepts the world as existing, and if I view that life exclusively as consciousness *of* the world, then I reveal myself as the pure ego with its pure stream of *cogitationes*.

I certainly do not discover myself as one item among others in the world, since I have altogether suspended judgment about ⟨9⟩ the world. / I am not the ego of an individual man. I am the ego in whose stream of consciousness the world itself — including myself as an object in it, a man who exists in the world — first acquires meaning and reality.

We have reached a dangerous point. It seems simple indeed to understand the pure ego with its *cogitationes* by following Descartes. And yet it is as if we were on the brink of a precipice, where the ability to step calmly and surely decides between philosophic life and philosophic death. Descartes was thoroughly sincere in his desire to be radical and presuppositionless. However, we know through recent researches — particularly the fine and penetrating work of Messrs. Gilson and Koyré — that a great deal of Scholasticism is hidden in Descartes' meditations as unarticulated prejudice. But this is not all. We must above all avoid the prejudices, hardly noticed by us, which derive from our emphasis on the mathematically oriented natural sciences. These prejudices make it appear as if the phrase *ego cogito* refers to an apodictic and primitive axiom, one which, in conjunction with others to be derived from it, provides the foundation for a deductive and universal science, a science *ordine geometrico*. In relation to this we must under no circumstances take for granted that, with our apodictic and pure ego, we have salvaged a small corner of the world as the single indubitable fact about the world which can be utilized by the philosophizing ego. It is not true that all that now remains to be done is to infer the rest of the world through correct deductive procedures according to principles that are innate to the ego.

Unfortunately, Descartes commits this error, in the apparently insignificant yet fateful transformation of the ego to a *substantia cogitans*, to an independent human *animus*, which then becomes the point of departure for conclusions by means of the principle of causality. In short, this is the transformation which made Descartes the father of the rather absurd transcendental realism. We will keep aloof from all this if we remain true to radicalism in our self-examination and with it to the principle of pure intuition. We must regard nothing as veridical except the pure immediacy and givenness in the field of the *ego cogito* which the *epoché* has opened up to us. In other words, we must not make assertions about that which we do not ourselves *see*. In these matters Descartes was deficient. It so happens that he stands before the greatest / of all discoveries — in a sense he has ⟨10⟩ already made it — yet fails to see its true significance, that of transcendental subjectivity. He does not pass through the gateway that leads into genuine transcendental philosophy.

The independent *epoché* with regard to the nature of the world as it appears and is real to me — that is, "real" to the previous and natural point of view — discloses the greatest and most magnificent of all facts: I and my life remain — in my sense of reality — untouched by whichever way we decide the issue of whether the world is or is not. To say, in my natural existence,

"I am, I think, I live," means that I am one human being among
others in the world, that I am related to nature through my
physical body, and that in this body my *cogitationes*, perceptions,
memories, judgments, etc. are incorporated as psycho-physical
facts. Conceived in this way, I, we, humans, and animals are
subject-matter for the objective sciences, that is, for biology,
anthropology, and zoology, and also for psychology. The life of
the psyche, which is the subject-matter of all psychology, is
understood only as the psychic life in the world. The methodology
of a purified Cartesianism demands of me, the one who philosophizes, the phenomenological *epoché*. This *epoché* eliminates
as wordly facts from my field of judgment both the reality of the
objective world in general and the sciences of the world. *Consequently, for me there exists no "I" and there are no psychic actions,*[1]
that is, psychic phenomena in the psychological sense. To myself
I do not exist as a human being, ⟨nor⟩ do my *cogitationes*
exist as components of a psycho-physical world. But through all
this I have discovered my true self. I have discovered that I
alone am the pure ego, with pure existence and pure capacities
(for example, the obvious capacity to abstain from judging).
Through this ego alone does *the being of the world*, and, for that
matter, any being whatsoever, make sense *to me* and has possible
validity. The world — whose conceivable non-being does not
extinguish my pure being but rather presupposes it — is termed
transcendent, whereas my pure being or my pure ego is termed
⟨11⟩ *transcendental*. Through the phenomenological *epo/ché* the natural human ego, specifically my own, is reduced to the transcendental ego. This is the meaning of the phenomenological
reduction.

Further steps are needed so that what has been developed up
to this point can be adequately applied. What is the philosophic
use of the transcendental ego? To be sure, for me, the one who
philosophizes, it obviously precedes, in an epistemological sense,
all objective reality. In a way, it is the basis for all objective
knowledge, be it good or bad. But does the fact that the transcendental ego precedes and presupposes all objective knowledge
mean also that it is an epistemological ground in the ordinary

[1] As a rule, "*Leistungen*" is here translated as "acts," and "*Akte*" as "actions."
(Tr.).

sense? The thought is tempting. All realistic theories are guilty of it. But the temptation to look in the transcendental subjectivity for premises guaranteeing the existence of the subjective world evanesces once we realize that all arguments, considered in themselves, exist already in transcendental subjectivity itself. Furthermore, all proofs for the world have their criteria set in the world just as it is given and justified in experience. However, these considerations must not be construed as a rejection of the great Cartesian idea that the ultimate basis for objective science and the reality of the objective world is to be sought in transcendental subjectivity. Otherwise — our criticisms aside — we would not be true to Descartes' method of meditation. However, the Cartesian discovery of the ego may perhaps open up a *new concept of foundation, namely, a transcendental foundation.*

In point of fact, instead of using the *ego cogito* merely as an apodictic proposition and as an absolutely primitive premise, we notice that the phenomenological *epoché* has uncovered for us (or for me, the one who philosophizes), through the apodictic *I am*, a new kind and an endless sphere of being. This is the sphere of a new kind of experience: transcendental experience. And herewith also arises the possibility of both transcendental epistemology and transcendental science.

A most extraordinary epistemological situation is disclosed / here. The phenomenological *epoché* reduces me to my transcen- ⟨12⟩ dental and pure ego. I am, thus, at least *prima facie*, in a certain sense *solus ipse*, but not in the ordinary sense, in which one might say that a man survived a universal holocaust in a world which itself remained unaffected. Once I have banished from my sphere of judgments the world, as one which receives its being from me and within me, then I, as the transcendental ego which is prior to the world, am *the sole source and object capable of judgment* [das einzig urteilsmäßig Setzbare und Gesetzte]. And now I am supposed to develop an unheard-of and unique science, since it is one that is created exclusively by and inside my transcendental subjectivity! Furthermore, this science is meant to apply, at least at the outset, to my transcendental subjectivity alone. It thus becomes a transcendental-solipsistic science. It is therefore not the *ego cogito*, but a science about the ego — a pure *egology* — which becomes the ultimate foundation of philosophy in the Cartesian sense of a universal science, and which must provide at least the cornerstone for its absolute foundation. In actual fact this science exists already as the lowest transcendental phenomenology. And I mean the lowest, not the fully developed phenomenology, because to the latter, of course, belongs the further development from transcendental solipsism to transcendental intersubjectivity.

To make all this intelligible it is first necessary to do what was neglected by Descartes, namely, to describe the endless field of the ego's transcendental experience itself. His own experience, as is well known, and especially when he judged it to be apodictic, plays a role in the philosophy of Descartes. But he neglected to describe the ego in the full concretion of its transcendental being and life, nor did he regard it as an unlimited work-project to be pursued systematically. It is an insight central to a philosopher that, by introducing the transcendental reduction, he can reflect truthfully on his *cogitationes* and on their pure phenomenological content. In this way he can uncover all aspects of his transcendental being with respect to both his transcendental-temporal life and also his capabilities. We are clearly dealing with a train of thought parallel to what the world-centered psychologist calls inner experience or experience of the self.

⟨13⟩ One thing of the greatest, even decisive, importance / remains. One cannot lightly dismiss the fact — even Descartes has so remarked on occasion — that the *epoché* changes nothing in the world. All experience is still his experience, all consciousness, still his consciousness. The expression *ego cogito* must be expanded by one term. Every *cogito* contains a meaning: its *cogitatum*. The experience of a house, as I experience it, and ignoring theories of perception, is precisely an experience of this and only this house, a house which appears in such-and-such a way, and has certain specific determinations when seen from the side, from near-by, and from afar. Similarly, a clear or a vague recollection is the recollection of a vaguely or clearly apprehended house. Even the most erroneous judgment means a judgment about such-and-such factual content, and so on. *The essence of consciousness, in which I live as my own self, is the so-called intention-*

ality. Consciousness is always consciousness of something. The nature of consciousness includes, as modes of being, presentations, probabilities, and non-being, and also the modes of appearance, goodness, and value, etc. Phenomenological experience as reflection must avoid any interpretative constructions. Its descriptions must reflect accurately the concrete contents of experience, precisely as these are experienced.

To interpret consciousness as a complex of sense data and then to bring forth gestalt-like qualities [*Gestaltqualitäten*] out of these — which are subsequently equated with the totality — is a sensualist invention. This interpretation is a basic error even from the worldly and psychological perspective, and much more so from the transcendental point of view. It is true that in the process of phenomenological analyses sense data do occur, and something is, in fact, disclosed about them. But what phenomenological analysis fails to find as primary is the "perception of an external world." The honest description of the unadulterated data of experience must disclose what appears first of all, *i.e.*, the *cogito*. For example, we must describe closely the perception of a house in terms of what it means as object and its modes of appearing. The same applies to all forms of consciousness.

When I focus on the object of consciousness I discover it as something which is experienced or meant as having such-and-such determinations. / When I judge, the object is the repository ⟨14⟩ of judgment-predicates; when I value, it is the repository of value-predicates. Looking the other way I discover the changing aspects of consciousness, *i.e.* that which is capable of perception and memory. This category comprises everything which is neither a physical object nor any determination of such an object. That is to say, it comprises the subjective mode of givenness or subjective mode of appearance, exemplified by perspective, or the distinction between vagueness and clarity, attention and inattention, etc.

To be a meditating philosopher who, through these meditations, has himself become a transcendental ego, and who constantly reflects about himself, means to enter upon often endless transcendental experience. It means to refuse to be satisfied with a vague *ego cogito* and instead pursue the steady flux of the *cogito* towards being and life. It means to see all that which is to be seen, to explain it and penetrate it, to encompass it descriptively by concepts and judgments. But these latter must only be terms which have been derived without alteration from their perceptual source.

As said before, the guiding schema for our exposition and description is a three-sided concept: *ego cogito cogitatum*. If we disregard for the time being the identical "I", notwithstanding that in a certain sense it resides in every *cogito*, then reflection will more readily disclose the various features of the *cogito* itself. Immediately there branch off descriptive types, only vaguely suggested by language, ⟨such as⟩ perceiving, remembering, still-being-conscious-of-the-recently-perceived, anticipating, desiring, willing, predicating, etc. Focusing on the concrete results of transcendental reflection brings out the fundamental distinction, already alluded to, between objective meaning and mode of consciousness, possible mode of appearance. That is, seen in essence, the reference here is to the two-sidedness which makes intentionality into consciousness as consciousness of such-and-such. This always yields two orientations for description.

In relation to the preceding we must thus call attention to the fact that the transcendental *epoché* performed with respect to the existing world, containing all those objects which we actually experience, perceive, remember, think, judge, and believe, does not change the fact that the world — *i.e.*, the objects as pure phenomena of experience, as pure *cogitata* of the momentary ⟨15⟩ *cogitationes* — must become a central concern / of phenomenological description. In that case, what is the nature of the abysmal difference between phenomenological judgments about the world of experience and natural-objective judgments? The answer can be given in these terms: as a phenomenological ego I have become a pure observer of myself. I treat as veridical only that which I encounter as inseparable from me, as pertaining purely to my life and being inseparable from it, exactly in the manner that genuine and intuitive reflection discloses my own self to me. Before the *epoché*, I was a man with the natural attitude and I lived immersed naively in the world. I accepted the experienced as such, and on the basis of it developed my subsequent positions. All this, however, took place in me wthouti my being aware of it. I was indeed interested in my experiences, that is, in objects, values, goals, but I did not focus on the experiencing of my life, on the act of being interested, on the act of taking a position, on my subjectivity. I was a transcendental ego even while in the living natural attitude, but I knew nothing about it. In order to become aware of my true being I needed to execute the phenomenological *epoché*. Through it I do not achieve — as Descartes attempted — a critique of validity, or, in other words, the resolution of the problem of the apodictic trustworthiness of my experience and consequently of the reality of the world. Quite to the contrary, I will learn that the world and how the world is for me the *cogitatum* of my *cogitationes*. I will not only discover that the *ego cogito* precedes apodictically the fact that the world exists for me, but also familiarize myself thoroughly with the concrete being of my ego and thereby *see* it. The being that I am when, immersed, I live and experience the world from the natural attitude consists of a particular transcendental life, namely, one in which I naively trust my experiences, one in which I continue to occupy myself with a naively acquired world view, etc. Therefore, the phenomenological attitude, with its *epoché*, consists in that *I reach the ultimate experiential and cognitive perspective thinkable. In it I become the disinterested spectator of my natural and wordly ego and its life.* In this manner, my natural life becomes merely one part or one particular level of what now has been disclosed as my transcendental life. I am detached inasmuch as I "suspend" all worldly interests (which I nonetheless possess), and to the degree that I — / the phi- ⟨16⟩ losophizing one — place myself above them and observe them, and take these as themes for description, as being my transcendental ego.

The phenomenological reduction thus tends to split the ego. The transcendental spectator places himself above himself, watches himself, and sees himself also as the previously world-immersed ego. In other words, he discovers that he, as a human being, exists within himself as a *cogitatum*, and, through the corresponding *cogitationes*, he discovers the transcendental life and being which make up ⟨the⟩ totality of the world. The natural man (in whom the ego, in the last analysis, is a transcendental one, but of which he knows nothing) possesses a world and a science which he naively takes to be absolute. However, the transcendental spectator who has reached the consciousness of a transcendental ego conceives the world merely as a *phenomenon*, that is, as the *cogitatum* of the momentary *cogitatio*, as the appearance of momentary appearances, as a mere correlate.

When phenomenology examines objects of consciousness — regardless of what kind, whether real or ideal — it deals with these exclusively as objects of the immediate consciousness. The description — which attempts to grasp the concrete and rich phenomena of the *cogitationes* — must constantly glance back from the side of the object to the side of consciousness and pursue the general existing connections. For example, if I consider the perception of a hexahedron, then I notice in pure reflection that the hexahedron is given as a continuous and unitary object together with a many-formed and determinate manifold of modes of appearance. It is the same hexahedron, the same appearance, regardless of whether viewed from this side or that one, from this or that perspective, from close or from afar, with greater or with lesser distinctness and determinateness. Nonetheless, if we see any hexahedral surface, any edge or corner, any spot of color, in short, any aspect of the objective sense, then we notice the same thing in every case: it is the unity of a manifold with constantly changing modes of appearance, a unity of its particular perspectives and of the particular differentiations of the subjective here and there. If we look uncritically we find a color that is always identical and unchanging. But if we reflect ⟨17⟩ on the mode in which it appears / we recognize that the color is nothing other, nor can it be thought as anything other, than that which presents itself now as this and now as that shade of color. Unity is always unity of representations, which is the representation of the spontaneous presentation of color or the presentation of an edge.

The *cogitatum* is possible only in the particular manner of the *cogito*. If we begin by taking the life of consciousness concretely and by persistently looking in all directions in order to describe its intentional and homogeneous traits, then a veritable infinity opens up, and constantly new and undreamed-of facts appear. To these belong the structures of phenomenological temporality. These structures already occur within the type of consciousness that is concerned with the perception of objects. This type of consciousness is alive, at any given moment, as duration, as the temporal and directional stream of the act of perceiving and the object perceived. This streaming progression, extension, or continuation, *i.e.*, temporality, is an essential element of the transcendental phenomenon itself. Any division that we may introduce yields, in turn, perceptions of the same type. We make the same assertions of each section and each phase: the hexahedron has been perceived. This *identity* is an immanent and descriptive trait of such an intentional experience and of its phases. It is a trait in consciousness itself. The pieces and phases of perception are not externally glued together; rather, they are unitary in the precise sense that one awareness is one with another awareness, that is to say, these are one because they are awareness of the same thing. It is not the case that first there are objects which are subsequently stuck into consciousness, in the sense that something is stuck in a certain place. On the contrary, one awareness ties itself with another, one *cogito* with another, by becoming a new *cogito* uniting both. This new *cogito*, being a new awareness, is in turn awareness of something. That we become aware of different events as one and the same is due to the activity of the *synthetic consciousness*.

Through an example we have hit upon synthesis as the unique and fundamental characteristic of consciousness. And through it also appeared the *distinction between real and ideal, that is, purely intentional, contents of consciousness*. The object of perception, considered phenomenologically, does not appear as a real thing either in per/ception or in the streaming perspectives that are ⟨18⟩ unified through synthesis, or in any other manifold of experience. Two appearances which, because of a synthesis, present themselves to me as appearances of the same thing are nonetheless really separate, and because of this separation they possess no datum in common; at the most, they have only related and similar traits. The hexahedron which one sees as one and the same is one and the same in intentionality. What appears as spatial reality, when examined as it is given in variegated perception, is identical in an ideational sense, that is, it is identical in intention; this identity is immanent in the modes of consciousness, in the acts of the ego, not as a real datum, but in the sense that it means an object. *The same* hexahedron may thus appear to me in a variety of recollections, expectations, or distinct or vacuous conceptions as intentionally the same; also, it can be the identical substratum for predications, valuations, etc. This identity always resides in consciousness proper and is apprehended through synthesis. *It follows that the stream of consciousness is permeated by the fact that consciousness relates itself to objects* [Gegenständlichkeit]. This relation is an essential characteristic of every act of consciousness. It is the ability to pass over — through synthesis — from perennially new and greatly disparate forms of consciousness to an awareness of their unity.

In this connection it is evident that the ego contains no individual isolated *cogito*. This is the case to such an extent that it is finally shown that all of existence — with its fluctuations, its Heraclitean flux — is one universal synthetic unity. It is because of this unity that we can say, not only that the transcendental ego exists, but that it exists for itself. The transcendental ego is a concrete unity that can be synoptically apprehended. It lives individualized in steadily new types of consciousness, yet it constantly objectifies itself as unitary through the form of immanent time.

This is not all. *Potentiality* in existence is just as important as *actuality*, and potentiality is not empty possibility. Every *cogito* — for instance, an external perception, a recollection, etc. — carries in itself a potentiality immanent to it and capable of being disclosed. It is a potentiality for possible experiences referring to the same intentional object, experiences which the ego can actualize. In each *cogito* we find, using phenomenological terminology, *horizons*, and in various senses. Perception occurs ⟨19⟩ and / sketches a horizon of expectations, which is a horizon of intentionality. The horizon anticipates the future as it might be perceived, that is to say, it points to coming series of perceptions. Each series, in turn, carries potentialities with it, such as the fact that I can look in one direction rather than another, and can redirect the run of my perceptions. Each recollection leads me to a long chain of possible recollections ending in the now; and at each point of immanent time it refers me to other present events that might be disclosed; and so on.

All these are intentional structures, and are governed by the laws of synthesis. I can question every intentional event, which means that I can penetrate and display its horizons. In doing this I disclose, on the one hand, potentialities of my existence, and on the other I clarify the intended meaning of objective reference.

Intentional analysis is thus something altogether different from analysis in the ordinary sense. The life of consciousness is neither a mere aggregate of data, nor a heap of psychic atoms, or a whole composed of elements united through gestalt-like qualities [*Gestaltqualitäten*]. This is true also of pure introspective psychology, as a parallel to transcendental phenomenology. *Intentional analysis is the disclosure of the actualities and potentialities in which objects constitute themselves as perceptual units.* Furthermore, all perceptual analysis takes place in the transition from real events to the intentional horizons suggested by them.

This late insight prescribes to phenomenological analysis and description an altogether new methodology. It is a methodology which goes into action whenever objects and meanings, questions about being, questions about possibilities, questions of origin, and questions of right are to be considered seriously. Every intentional analysis reaches beyond the immediately and actually [*reell*] given events of the immanent sphere, and in such a way that the analysis discloses potentialities — which are now given actually [*reell*] and whose horizons have been sketched — and brings out manifold aspects of new experiences in which are made manifest what earlier was meant only implicitly and in this way was already present intentionally. When I see a hexahedron I say, in reality and in truth I see it only from one side. It is nonetheless evident / that what I now ⟨20⟩ experience is in reality more. The perception includes a non-sensory belief through which the visible side can be understood to be a mere side in the first place. But how does this belief, that there is more, disclose itself? How does it become obvious that I mean more? It occurs through the transition to a synthetic sequence of possible perceptions, perceptions I would have — as indeed I can — were I to walk around the object. Phenomenology always explains meanings, that is, intentionality, by producing these sense-fulfilling syntheses. The tremendous task placed on description is to expound the universal structure of transcendental consciousness in its reference to and creation of meanings.

Naturally, the research develops on different levels. Our research is not hindered by the fact that its province is the realm of subjective flux and that it would be madness to proceed in terms of a method of concept- and judgment-formation that is appropriate to the objective and exact sciences. True enough, the life of consciousness is in flux, and every *cogito* is fluid, that is, devoid of fixed last elements and ultimate relations. But the flux is governed by a highly pronounced class structure. Perception is a general class, recollection is another class; a further class is a kind of "conscious vacuum with a memory," exemplified by a portion of a melody which I no longer hear but *still* have within my field of consciousness, a melody which is not perceived yet refers to a particular melody. These are illustrations of universal, sharply pronounced classes which in turn instantiate themselves in the psychophysical being as the class of the *perceptions of all spatial objects* and the class of the *perceptions of human beings*.

I can question each class — described in general terms — about its structure, and, to be sure, about its intentional structure, since it is an intentional class. I can ask how one class overlaps onto another, how it is formed, inflected, what forms of intentional synthesis reside in it necessarily, what kinds of horizons are contained in it necessarily, what types of disclosure and types of fulfillment belong to it. This results in a transcendental theory of perception, that is, in an intentional analysis of perception, in a transcendental theory of recollection and of the inter- /
⟨21⟩ connections of intuitions in general, and also in a transcendental theory of jugdment, theory of volition, etc. The important distinction is that we must not — as is the case with the objective factual sciences — concern ourselves with pure experience and give a realistic [*reell*] analysis of the datum of experience, but follow the lines of intentional synthesis, as these are indicated in terms of their intentionality and horizons. In this manner we must exhibit and disclose the horizons themselves.

Each individual *cogitatum* — since it is stretched out in time in a transcendental and immanent manner — is a synthesized identity, that is, an awareness of the continuity of the same event. As a consequence, an individual object already functions, in a sense, as a transcendental clue to the subjective multiplicities that constitute the object. But when we survey the most general classes of *cogitata* and their general intentional description, then it is immaterial to which of several objects we refer, and whether these objects are perceived or remembered, and so forth.

The situation is quite different, however, when we consider the phenomenon of *world*, that astonishing genus "universal awareness of the world." As in other cases, we are aware that — within the synthetic and unitary flow of perceptions — this genus is a unity. We ask how the fact that there exists a world for us is to be understood intentionally. We focus consistently, as *cogitatum*, naturally, on the synthetic object-class called *world*, and view it as *the clue for unfolding the structure of infinity which is present in the intentionality of experience when it refers to the world*. Herewith we arrive at the question of individuals. The world of experience, considered through the phenomenological reduction purely as experienced, is organized into identical and persisting objects. What is the nature of that particular infinity which pertains to the actual and possible perception of objects? The same question applies to every class of objects. What is the intentional structure of the horizon without which an object cannot be an object? This intentionality points to the cohesion of the world, without which — as is shown by the analysis of intentionality proper — no object can be thought. These considerations apply to every class of objects which could possibly belong to the world.

The conceptual [*ideelle*] fixation of an intentional object-class leads, in intentional researches, as one soon recognizes, to an organization or order. / In other words, transcendental sub- ⟨22⟩ jectivity is not a chaos of intentional experiences, but it is a unity through synthesis. It is a many-levelled synthesis in which always new classes and individuals are constituted. However, every object expresses a *rule structured within transcendental subjectivity*.

We are inquiring into the transcendental system of intentionality. Through it, nature or the world exist invariably for the ego — first in experience, as directly visible and tangible intentionality, and later as any other kind of intentionality directed towards the world. This question places us in the phenomenology of reason [*Vernunft*]. Reason and unreason, understood in the widest sense, do not represent accidentally actual capacities and facts, but pertain to the universal structure of transcendental subjectivity.

Evidence, in its widest sense of something "showing itself," — as something that "stands there as itself," or being cognizant of a matter of fact, a value, and the like — is no accidental occurrence in transcendental existence. On the contrary, intentionality is either itself an awareness of evidence — a characteristic of the *cogitatum* itself — or it is applied and directed (essentially and in the manner of a horizon) to "authentic givenness" [*Selbstgebung*]. Every clarification is already a way of making evident. Every vague, empty, and unclear act of awareness is, from the outset, awareness of such-and-such only insofar as it *points the way to clarification*, in which what is meant is to be given either as a reality or as a possibility. I can inquire of each vague awareness what its object must look like. Of course, one aspect of the structure of transcendental subjectivity is that occasionally opinions are formed which — as these proceed, in their actual progress in experience, towards possible evidence (*i.e.*, towards clear presentation) from a belief to the evidential matter of fact — do not disclose that which was meant as a possible individual, but disclose something else. Instead of confirmation and fulfillment we often find disappointment, dissolution, and negation. All this is typical of the realm of consciousness, with its antithetical occurrences of fulfillment ⟨23⟩ and disappointment. / The ego always and necessarily exists in *cogitationes*, and the presented object is always either visible — in awareness (if it is) or in phantasy (as if it were) — or non-visible, removed from the facts. One can always ask what the procedures are that decide whether an object is real or illusory, and also, about the procedures through which we can consistently reach an object's existential disclosure and can be assured of unanimous continuity in the evidence. Or, finally, we ask after the procedures which might, instead, demonstrate the non-being of the sought object.

An object exists for me; that is to say, it has reality for me in consciousness. But this reality is reality for me only as long as I believe that I can confirm it. By this I mean that I must be able to provide usable procedures, that is, procedures which run through automatically, and other evidences, which lead me then to the object itself and through which I realize the object as being *truly there*. The same holds when my awareness of the object is a matter of experience, that is, when my awareness tells me that the object itself is already there, that the object itself is seen. This act of seeing, in turn, points to further seeing, that is, it points to the possibility of confirmation. Finally, it points to the fact that what has already once been realized as being can nonetheless be restored, again and again, to its previous condition of progressive confirmation.

Think about the tremendous importance of this remark, considering that we are on an egological foundation. We can see, from this ultimate point of view, that existence and essence have for us, in reality and truth, no other meaning than that of possible confirmation. Furthermore, these confirmation-procedures and their accessibility belong to me as transcendental subjectivity and make sense only as such.

True being, therefore, whether real or ideal, *has significance only as a particular correlate of my own intentionality,* actual or potential. Of course, this is not true of an isolated *cogito*. For example, the being of a real thing is not the mere *cogito* of an isolated perception that I now have. But the perception and its intentionally given object call to my attention, by virtue of the presumed horizon, an endless and open system of *possible* per- / ceptions, perceptions which are not invented but which are ⟨24⟩ motivated from within my intentional existence, and which can lose their presumed validity only when conflicting experience eliminates it. These possible perceptions are necessarily presupposed as *my* possibilities, ones which I can bring about — provided I am not hindered — by approaching the object, looking around it, etc.

Needless to say, the foregoing has been stated very crudely. Extremely far-reaching and complex intentional analyses are needed in order to explain the structure of these possibilities as they relate to the specific horizons belonging to every individual class of objects, and to clarify therewith the meaning of actual being. At the outset only one fact is evident and guides me, namely, that I accept as being only that which presents itself to me as being, and that all conceivable justification of it lies within my own self and is determined in my immediate and mediate intentionality, in which any other meaning of being is also to be determined.

We are thus confronted with the great — indeed, the overwhelmingly great — problem of *reason and reality*, of consciousness and true being. In phenomenology these problems are referred to as *constitutive problems*. At first sight these questions appear to be limited phenomenological problems, since one is apt to think of reality or being exclusively in terms of wordly being. Consequently, one is likely to think of a parallel between phenomenology and the common and so-called theory of knowledge or critique of reason, which usually refers to knowledge of objective reality. In reality, however, constitutive problems encompass the complete transcendental phenomenology and define a wholly universal and systematic aspect under which all phenomenological problems are ordered. By phenomenological constitution of an object is meant the view of the ego's universality from the perspective of the identity of this object. That is to say, it is reflection on the question of the systematic totality of real and possible conscious experiences, which — while they refer to an object — are nonetheless anticipated in my ego and represent to me a strict rule for possible syntheses.

The problem of the phenomenological constitution of any class of objects is first the problem of the ideally [*ideal*] complete ⟨25⟩ and evident givenness of that class. Every class / of objects possesses a typical kind of possible experiences. What are the essential structures of these experiences, in particular when we think of them as disclosing the object, ideally [*ideal*], completely and from every point of view? To it we must add the following question: how does it happen that the ego has in its possession and at its disposal such a system, when there is no actual experience of it? Finally, what is the significance to me of the fact that some objects are for me exactly what they are, when in reality I neither have now nor have had in the past any knowledge of them?

Every existing object belongs to a universe of possible experiences. In this connection we need only broaden the concept of experience to its most comprehensive, which is that of properly understood evidence. To every possible object there corresponds such a possible system. As already stated, we call "transcendental" the progressing object-index which is part of a very definite yet universal structure belonging to the ego. It is a progression which advances towards the ego's real *cogitata* as well as towards potentialities and capacities. But ⟨it⟩ is the nature of the ego to exist in the form of real and possible awareness. Its possibilities depend on the various patterns of the *I can,* of the capacities which reside within the ego's own subjectivity. The ego is what it is solely in reference to intentional objectivities; it always possesses that which is and that which has the possibility of being. Consequently, the essential characteristic of the ego is persistently to form systems of intentionality, as well as to possess systems already formed, whose indices are the objects which the ego means, thinks, values, handles, imagines, or could possibly imagine, and so forth.

But the ego itself has being, and its being is being for itself. Also, its being, together with all that specifically belongs to it, is constituted in the ego and continues to constitute itself for the ego. The ego's being-for-itself is being that is in a state of continual self-constitution, which, in turn, is the foundation for all constitution of so-called transcendentals, *i.e.*, worldly objectivities. It is thus the basis of constitutive phenomenology to create — by means of the doctrine of the constitution of immanent temporality and that of its subordinate *immanent* events — an egological theory, so that through this theory we can then understand, step by step, *how the ego's being-for-itself is concretely possible and understandable.* |

We now have to face an ambiguity in the notion of the ego: ⟨26⟩ it is a different ego on each of various levels of phenomenological problems. In the first and most general structural considerations we find, as a result of phenomenological reduction, the *ego cogito cogitata*. We are struck with the manifoldness of *cogitata,* such as we find in *I perceive, I remember, I desire,* etc. It is above all important to notice that the many modes of the *cogito* possess a point of identity, a center, in the fact that I — always the same I — am the one who carries out now the act of thinking, then the act of evaluating something as appearance, etc. A double synthesis, a double polarization, becomes apparent. Many, but not all, of the modes of awareness that elapse are synthetically united as modes of awareness of the same object. On the other side, however, all *cogitationes*, and primarily all my points of view, have the structural pattern, *(ego) cogito*. They possess the ego-polarization.

But now we must observe that the central ego is not an empty point or pole, but that, in virtue of the rules of genesis, it experiences, with each act that radiates from the ego, a lasting determination. For example, should I have decided the nature of something through an act of judgment, then this fleeting act disappears, but I do remain the ego which has thus decided. I find myself continuous [*selbst*] and enduring, as the ego of my enduring convictions. The same applies to every kind of decision, as for example decisions regarding value and volition.

The ego is thus not merely an empty pole, but the permanent and enduring subject of persisting convictions and habits through whose alterations *the unity of the personal ego and its personal character is* first *constituted*. From this we must dissociate the ego in its full concretion, because the ego is concrete only in the flowing multiplicity of its intentional existence and with the objects that are meant and constituted for it therein. The ego may thus also be viewed as a concrete monad.

I, as transcendental ego, apprehend myself as an ego in one of the above senses and am capable of familiarizing myself with my true and real being. Consequently, this fact also is ⟨a constitutive⟩ problem, and indeed, the most radical constitutive problem. /

⟨27⟩   In truth, constitutive phenomenology encompasses all of phenomenology. However, the latter cannot begin as constitutive phenomenology, but must set out with an analysis of the classes of awareness and their intentional development. And only later does the analysis make apparent the meaning of constitutive problems.

Nonetheless, the phenomenological problems which analyze the nature of the constitution of the ego's real [*realen*] objectivities, and with it the analysis of a phenomenologically objective epistemology, form a sizable realm by themselves.

But before we can confront this epistemology with the ordinary one, extraordinary methodological progress is required. I reach this progress late in order to allow the concretions to speak to you unencumbered. Every one of us who has been guided back, through phenomenological reduction, to *his* absolute ego discovered himself, with apodictic certainty, as an actual existent. Looking around, the ego discovered diverse classes — classes which can be fixed descriptively and developed intentionally — and could soon proceed to the intentional disclosure of its own ego. But it was no accident that the expressions "essence" and "essential" [*wesensmäßig*] escaped me repeatedly. These expressions are equivalent to a definite concept of the a priori, a concept clarified only by phenomenology. It is clear that if we explain and describe a class of *cogitata*, such as perceptions, *qua* class — such as the perceived, retention and the retained, recollection and the recollected, assertion and the asserted, seeking and the sought, etc. — then we are led to results which persist regardless of how we abstract from actual facts. The individuality of the instantiating actuality — as for instance the present flux of perceptions of the table — is completely irrelevant to the class. Equally irrelevant are the general impressions which I — the actual ego — acquire in my experiences of this class. The description does not depend on discovering individual facts or establishing their existence. The same holds for all egological structures.

An analysis of the class of sensible and spatially objective experiences may serve as example. I proceed systematically to the constitutive problem of how such experience would have to unfold itself consistently so that one and the same object might disclose itself completely, *i.e.*, with all its intended attributes. / It is then that I hit upon the great realization that ⟨28⟩ before anything can be, for me, a truly existing object, it must fulfill certain necessary a priori conditions. It must appear in the form of a specific and relevant structural system dealing with experiential possibilities. An object appears with a multiplicity of specifically related structures that is determined a priori.

Evidently I am quite free in what I may imagine my ego to be. I may view the classes as pure ideal [*ideale*] possibilities of the now merely possible ego, or of any possible ego whatsoever (as a free interpretation of my actual being). In this manner I reach *classes of essences, a priori possibilities, and corresponding essential laws of being* [Wesensgesetze]. The same applies to general structures of the essence [*Wesensstrukturen*] of my ego insofar as it can be thought of at all. Without these structures I can neither conceive of my self in general nor a priori, because they evidently and necessarily must have a certain configuration for every free inflection of my ego.

We have reached a methodological insight which, next to the genuine method of phenomenological reduction, is the most important in phenomenology: *the ego*, to use traditional language, *possesses an enormous inborn a priori*. All of phenomenology, or the methodical pursuit of a philosopher's self-examination, discloses the endless multiformity of this inborn a priori. This is the genuine sense of "innate," a sense that the older and naive concept searched thoroughly, as it were, but was unable to grasp.

There is much more to the inborn a priori of the concrete ego — to *my monad*, using Leibniz' expression — than we could discuss here. To this a priori belongs — and we can touch upon it only briefly — the a priori of the "I" in the particular sense that determines the universal triad of the term *cogito*. In other words, the ego is a pole in all specific perspectives or ego-acts; the ego is also the pole of the affects which — proceeding from objects that are already constituted — unfailingly motivate it to look attentively and to take a perspective. The ego thus possesses a double polarization: the polarization that is directed towards manifold objective unities, and the "I"-polarization, a centralization by virtue of which all intentionalities are related to the identical "I"-pole. /

⟨29⟩   But in a certain sense the "I"-polarization is multiplied within the ego, indirectly, by empathy with certain confrontations which occur within the ego itself, and which are the reflections of other monads, with, in turn, other "I"-poles. The "I" is not merely the pole of perspectives which come and go; every perspective leaves a residue in the "I", a tentative *conviction*.

The systematic explanation of the transcendental sphere interpreted as the absolute sphere of being and constitution is of extraordinary difficulty. Everything conceivable is rooted in this sphere. It has only been within the last decade that methodologies and the layers of the problems have clearly fallen into place.

The access to problems of the universal lawfulness of phenomenological genesis appeared rather late, and disclosed at bottom a *passive genesis*, instrumental in the formation of new intentionalities and apperceptions, yet without any active participation of the "I". In this connection a phenomenology of association was developed. Its conception and origin received a fundamentally new form through the at first surprising realization that "association" is a monstrous name for lawfulness, that is, for an inborn a priori, without which ⟨the⟩ ego as such is unthinkable. On the other side, the problems of *the higher-level* genesis were developed, in which reality-formations [*Geltungsgebilde*] proceed from "I"-acts, and in which the central "I" takes on specific "I"-characteristics, as for example habitual convictions and acquired characteristics.

Only through a phenomenology of genesis can the ego be understood as an infinite cohesion of synthetically connected *acts*, which are constitutive and always realize new levels of existing objects at various levels of relativity. We can then understand how the ego is only what it is by a genesis through which it incessantly appropriates intentionally, temporarily or permanently, both real and ideal [*reale und ideale*] existing worlds. The ego appropriates these worlds from its own sensory creations. It appropriates them under a priori possible and intervening corrections, deletions of unrealities, appearances, etc., which likewise arise as immanent and typical sensory events. The actual facts of experience are / irrational, but their ⟨30⟩ form — the enormous formal system of constituted objects and the correlative formal system of their intentional a priori constitution — consists of an inexhaustibly infinite a priori. Phenomenology explores this a priori, which is nothing other than the essence [*Wesensform*] of the ego *qua* ego, and which is disclosed, and can only be disclosed, by means of my own self-examination.

To the acts, which constitute meaning and being, belong all levels of reality, such as, for instance, ideas, as when we count and calculate, when we describe nature and the world, or treat them theoretically, when we form propositions, inferences, proofs, theories, or develop these into truths, etc. In this way we persistently create for ourselves new configurations of objects, in this case ideal objects, which for us have lasting reality. If we engage in radical self-examination — that is, return to our ego, every one for himself to his absolute ego — then all these forms are seen to be creations of spontaneous "I"-activity, and ⟨are⟩ classified under the category of egological constitution. Every ideal [*ideal*] being of this sort is what it is only as index of its constitutive systems. There we also find all the sciences, which, through my own thinking and perceiving, I bring to reality within myself. As an ego, I have suspended the naive acceptance of the sciences. However, in connection with my transcendental self-clarification as the non-participating spectator of my acts and life [*leistenden Leben*], the sciences and the world of experience are reaffirmed, but this time only as constitutive correlates.

We now proceed to relate this egological and transcendental theory of the constitution of being — a theory which shows that whatever exists for the ego arose from the synthesizing motives which are at the basis of the constructions effected by the passive and active acts of the ego's own intentional life — to the usual *theory of knowledge* or *theory of reason*. However, we still lack a cornerstone of phenomenological theory, for we need something that neutralizes the appearance of solipsism that is here given. This problem first becomes serious in a larger context; consequently, we may deal with it in passing and thus overcome this stumbling block.

The problem of traditional epistemology is that of *transcendence*. Epistemology, even though it purports to be empirical because it rests on ordinary psychology, does not intend to be a mere psychology of knowledge, but to explain the possibility of knowledge in the first place. The problem of epistemology arises
⟨31⟩ from within the natural or ordinary perspective [*Einstellung*] / and continues to be analyzed in that same perspective. I discover myself as a human being in the world, as one who at the same time experiences that world, and as one who knows it scientifically — and this scientific knowledge includes me. I now say to

myself: all that which exists for me exists by virtue of my cognitive consciousness; everything is for me the experienced of my experiencing, the thought of my thinking, the theorized of my theorizing, the intuited of my intuiting. Everything that is exists for me only as the intentional objectivity of my *cogitationes*. Intentionality as the fundamental characteristic of my psychic life designates a genuine peculiarity which belongs to me as a human being, as it belongs to every human being by virtue of his purely psychic inwardness. Already Brentano moved intentionality into the center of empirical psychology. This requires no phenomenological reduction; we are and we remain grounded on the given world. And so we say, understandably, that *everything which is and has reality for me, that is, for man, exists only in my own consciousness*, a consciousness which remains with itself in every awareness of a world and in all scientific activity. Any distinctions that I draw between veridical and illusory experience, and between reality and appearance, occur themselves within my own sphere of consciousness. The same is true even when, at a higher level, I distinguish between intelligent and unintelligent thinking, between what is necessary a priori and what is contradictory, and what is empirically true and what is empirically false. Evidently real, logically necessary [*denknotwendig*], contradictory, logically possible [*denkmöglich*], probable, etc., all these, appearing in my realm of consciousness itself, are characteristics of the actual intentional object. Every proof or foundation for truth and being takes place entirely in my own self; its product is a characteristic in the *cogitatum* of my *cogito*.

We now see the great problem. That, in connection with the motive for certitude which determines me, I reach conclusive evidences within my realm of consciousness is understandable enough. However, how can this game, which takes place in the purely immanent life of consciousness, acquire *objective* significance? How is it possible for evidence (the *clara et distincta perceptio*) to claim to be more than a mere aspect of my own consciousness? It is the Cartesian problem, which was meant to have been solved by the divine *veracitas*. |

Of what relevance here is the transcendental self-examination ⟨32⟩ of phenomenology? Nothing other than that it shows the entire problem to be contradictory. Descartes fell for this contradiction merely because he missed the true meaning of the transcendental *epoché* and that of the reduction to the pure ego. The usual post-Cartesian perspective [*Einstellung*] is even cruder. We ask, who is this "I" that can rightfully ask transcendental questions? As a natural human being, can I seriously ask, and ask in a transcendental sense, questions such as, "How can I go beyond the island that is my consciousness? How can that which appears in my consciousness as an experience of evidence acquire objective significance?" *To the extent that I apprehend myself as a natural human being, I presuppose having apprehended a spatial reality* [Raumwelt]; I have conceived of myself as being in space, in which I consequently have an outside of myself! Is it not true that the meaning of the question presupposes the validity of the perception of the world, whereas in fact, and conversely, this objective validity should appear as the reply to the question? The deliberate execution of the *phenomenological reduction* is necessary in order *to reach that "I"* and that conscious state [*Bewußtseinsleben*] *to which the transcendental questions, as questions about the possibility of transcendental knowledge, must be directed.* Rather than carry out a superficial phenomenological *epoché*, if one proceeds to disclose, through systematic self-examination and as pure ego, his entire realm of consciousness, that is, himself, then he recognizes that everything which exists for the ego is constituted in the ego itself. Furthermore, he recognizes that every mode of being, including those characterized as transcendent, has its particular constitution.

Transcendence is an immanent mode of being, that is, one that constitutes itself within the ego. Every conceivable meaning, every thinkable being — regardless of whether it is immanent or transcendent — falls within the realm of transcendental subjectivity. The idea of something outside of this realm is a contradiction: transcendental subjectivity is the universal and absolute concretion. To conceive of the universe of true being as being something outside of the universe of possible consciousness, of possible knowledge, and of possible evidence — with both universes being related merely externally through an inflexible /
⟨33⟩ law — is sheer nonsense. Essentially both belong together; and what belongs together essentially is a concrete unity, one in

absolute concretion: that of *transcendental subjectivity*. Transcendental subjectivity is the universe of possible meanings; any externality to it is meaningless. However, every bit of nonsense has its own mode of meaning and shows that it is nonsense precisely in that it can be examined and comprehended. However, these considerations do not apply to the mere *factual ego* and to what is factually accessible to it as existing for it; phenomenological self-disclosure is an a priori activity, and, consequently, applies to any possible and conceivable ego, and to any conceivable existent, *i.e.*, to all conceivable worlds.

Consequently, a genuine theory of knowledge makes sense only when it is transcendental and phenomenological. In that case it does not deal with meaningless conclusions from an alleged immanence to an alleged transcendence, the so-called *things-in-themselves*, but instead deals exclusively with the systematic exposition and clarification of the act of knowledge. By means of this clarification the act of knowledge is understood, through and through, as an intentional act. In this way, every type of being, whether real [*reales*] or ideal [*ideales*], is understood as a formation which is constituted in this particular act of transcendental subjectivity. This type of understanding is the highest conceivable form of rationality. All erroneous interpretations of being originate in a naive blindness for the horizons which co-determine the meaning of being. The ego's genuine self-disclosure — carried through in careful evidence and hence concretely — leads to a *transcendental idealism*, but one in a fundamentally *new sense*. It is not a psychological idealism. It is not an idealism which purports to derive a meaningful world from meaningless sense data. Nor is it a Kantian idealism, which, by being a limiting conception, had hoped to leave open the possibility for a world of things-in-themselves. *Our idealism is nothing other than a consistently carried through self-disclosure,* that is, *in the form of a systematic egological science,* of any meaning of being which makes sense to me, the ego. This idealism is not the construction of playful arguments; it is not as if we were engaged in a dialectical struggle with realisms, where idealism is the prize / that must be won. It is an idealism, rather, ⟨34⟩ which follows from a genuinely worked-out analysis of meanings as these appear (to the ego in experience) in the transcendence of nature, of culture, and of the world in general, which is, in turn, the systematic disclosure of the constituting intentionality itself. The proof for this idealism is found in the active exercise of phenomenology itself.

We must now deal with the one thought that is truly disturbing. If I, the meditating "I", reduce myself through an *epoché* to my absolute ego and to that which constitutes itself therein, then, do I not become the *solus ipse?* Did not then this whole philosophy of self-examination turn out to be pure solipsism, even though a transcendental and phenomenological solipsism?

Before we decide and seek to help ourselves with useless dialectic arguments, we must engage in the broad and systematic phenomenological task of exploring how, in the ego, the *alter ego* manifests and confirms itself as an experienced presentation. We must ask what kind of constitution is necessary for another self to appear as an existent in my realm of consciousness and in my world. It is a fact that I experience other minds as real, and not only do I experience them in conjunction with nature, but as interlaced into one whole with nature. Furthermore, I experience other minds in a unique manner. Not only do I experience them as spatial presentations psychologically interlaced with the realm of nature, but I also experience them as experiencing this selfsame world which I experience. I also experience them as experiencing me in the same way that I experience them, and so on. In myself, within the confines of my transcendental consciousness, I experience everything whatsoever. But I experience the world not as my own private world, but as an intersubjective world, one that is given to all human beings and which contains objects accessible to all. In it others exist as others, as well as for each other, as being there for anyone. How can we account for the inexplicable fact that everything which exists for me can acquire meaning and verification in my intentional existence?

Here we need a genuine phenomenological description of the transcendental act of *empathy*. With it, as long as it has been called in question, we require an abstractive suspension of other minds and of all those experiential levels of my world which /
⟨35⟩ originate from the belief in the existence of other minds. In doing this, the specific private egological being — my concrete selfhood

— is isolated within the realm of the transcendental ego, *i.e.*, within its realm of consciousness, as one with whose analogues I can achieve empathy through the motivations springing from my own ego. I experience my own conscious existence directly and truly as *it itself*. This is not true of the consciousness of others, such as their sensations, perceptions, thinking, feeling, desiring. In my own self, however, these experiences of others appear in a secondary sense, as "co-experienced," ⟨*i.e.*⟩ in the mode of a unique perception of similarity. These experiences show consistency in their indices and in this manner confirm themselves unanimously. We can say, with Leibniz, that within the *monad* which is given to me apodictically and originally are the reflections of alien monads. These reflections are confirmed consistently. However, what is indicated under these circumstances, that is, when I carry out phenomenological self-disclosure and through it the interpretation of what is legitimately indicated, is another transcendental subjectivity. The transcendental ego establishes in itself — not arbitrarily, but necessarily — a transcendental *alter ego*.

In this manner, transcendental subjectivity is expanded to become *intersubjectivity, to become an intersubjective transcendental community,*[1] *which, in turn, is the transcendental ground for the intersubjectivity of nature and of the world in general*, and, no less, of the intersubjective being of all ideal objectivities. The first ego to which the transcendental reduction leads us is still devoid of the distinction between, on the one hand, the intentionality which belongs to it originally, and, on the other hand, that which is in it the *reflection* of the *alter ego*. Before we can reach and recognize intersubjectivity as transcendental we need a highly developed and concrete phenomenology. But all this demonstrates that, for the one who meditates philosophically, his ego is the original ego, and that, further, intersubjectivity, for every conceivable ego as *alter ego*, makes sense only as reflection in that ego. In this exposition of empathy we notice a profound difference between the constitution of nature — which already makes sense to the abstractly isolated ego, although it does not

---

[1] *Sozialität* could have been rendered "sociality"; however, the word Husserl used in the *Cartesianische Meditationen* for a similar meaning is the improved term, *Gemeinschaft*, which is properly translated as "community." (Tr.)

yet make any intersubjective sense — and the constitution of the mental world. /

⟨36⟩ *Phenomenological idealism thus reveals itself as a transcendental and phenomenological monadology*, one which is not a metaphysical construction, but a systematic explanation of the meaning that the world has for all of us prior to any philosophizing. This pre-philosophic meaning can be distorted, but it cannot be changed, by philosophy.

The entire path we have traversed is supposed to be one directed by the unwavering Cartesian goal of a universal philosophy, that of a universal science grounded on an absolute foundation. We can say that he could have truly consummated his intention; and we see that his goal can really be carried out.

Daily and practical existence is naive; it is the immersion in an already-given world and consists of experiencing, thinking, valuing, acting. All those intentional acts of experience through which objects simply exist are carried out anonymously; the experiencer knows nothing of them. He is equally ignorant of his active thought: the numbers, the predicate states of affairs, the values, the purposes, the works, all these appear, thanks to the hidden acts. These presentations construct themselves, member upon member; they alone are visible. It is no different with the positive sciences. The latter are naivetés of a higher order; they are constructions of an intelligent and theoretical technology, but they do not explain the intentional acts from which ultimately everything originates.

Science, however, claims that its theoretical steps are justifiable, and depends everywhere on criticism. The *criticism we have in science*, however, *is not the ultimate critique of knowledge*. That would be the study and criticism of the original acts, the disclosure of all their intentional horizons — in terms of which one can ultimately understand the range of evidences, and correlatively evaluate the existential meaning of objects, of theoretical constructs, of values, and of purposes. As a consequence we find, in particular at the high level of the modern positive sciences, problems of foundation, paradoxes, and incomprehensibilities. The *basic concepts* which, in science, determine the meaning of its sphere of objects, of its theories, and which are common to all the sciences, *originate in a naive manner*.

These concepts have undetermined intentional horizons; / they ⟨37⟩
are constructions of intentional acts that are unknown and
exercised only with crude naiveté. This criticism applies not only
to positive and specialized sciences, but also to traditional logic
with all its formal norms. Every attempt to move from sciences
that have become historically established onto a better foundation — to arrive at meanings and acts by means of a better
self-understanding — is merely one item of self-examination on
the part of the scientist. But there is only *one* type of radical
self-examination, and that is the phenomenological one. Radical
self-examination and completely universal self-examination are
inseparable, and, concurrently, inseparable from the genuine
phenomenological method of self-examination when applied to
the essential totality of beings. Universal and essential self-
disclosure, however, implies command over all the ideal possibilities that are *inborn* both in the ego and in a transcendental
intersubjectivity.

A phenomenology that is carried out consistently constructs
a priori — yet with strictly intuited essential necessity and
generality — the *forms of conceivable worlds*, and again ⟨con-
structs⟩ these worlds themselves within the limits of all thinkable forms of being and by their system of stratification. This
is done in an original way, that is, in correlation with the constitutive a priori and with the intentional acts that constitute them.

Phenomenological procedure possesses no antecedent realities
or conceptions of reality, but instead, from the very beginning,
creates its concepts through original acts — which in turn are
fixed in original concepts. Furthermore, phenomenology, because
of its necessity to disclose all horizons, governs all differences of
range and all abstract relativities. Consequently, phenomenology
must arrive from within itself at those conceptual systems which
determine the fundamental meaning of scientific constructions.
These are the concepts that trace out all formal demarcations
of the idea of a possible world, and, consequently, must be the
genuine foundation-concepts of all knowledge. For such concepts
there can be no paradoxes.

The same holds for all those fundamental concepts which
apply to the construction and the total structural pattern of the
sciences that refer, and can refer, to various regions of being.

We can now say the following: in the last analysis, all a priori
sciences spring from within a priori and transcendental phe-
⟨38⟩ nomenology / because of its search for correlations. Granting this
origin, the sciences are parts of a universal and a priori phenomenology in the sense of being its systematic ramifications.
Consequently, this system of the universal a priori must also be
defined as the systematic development of the universal a priori
which is inborn in the nature of transcendental subjectivity and
intersubjectivity. It may further be defined as the systematic
development of *the universal logos of all conceivable being*. In
other words, a systematically and fully developed transcendental
phenomenology is *ipso facto the true and genuine universal
ontology*. It is not a vacuous and formal ontology, but one which
includes all the regional possibilities of being and all their corresponding correlations.

This universal and concrete ontology (also the universal logic
of being) is therefore the first universe of science based on
absolute proof. In proper succession, the intrinsically first
philosophic discipline would be a *solipsistically* restricted egology.
After that, through expansion, comes the intersubjective
phenomenology, but in a generality which first of all deals with
universal questions, and then ramifies itself into the a priori
sciences.

This universal a priori is then *the foundation for genuine
sciences of matters of fact* and *for a genuinely universal philosophy
in the Cartesian sense: a universal science based on absolute proof*.
All rationality pertaining to actual facts resides in the a priori.
A priori science is the science of the essential, that upon which
the science of matters of fact must return for it to be ultimately
and essentially grounded. However, a priori science must not be
naive, but must spring forth from ultimate transcendental and
phenomenological sources.

Finally, I wish to point out — so as to avoid misunderstandings
— that phenomenology excludes only that type of metaphysics
which deals with naive and contradictory objects, but it does not
exclude metaphysics altogether. The intrinsically first type of
being, that which precedes and bears every worldly objectivity,
⟨39⟩ is transcendental inter/subjectivity, consisting of the various
manifestations of the total community of monads. But inside the

factual monadic sphere — and as ideal and essential possibilities in every conceivable monadic sphere — arise all the problems of contingency, death, destiny, of the possibility of a meaningful individual and communal life, that is, arise also the problems of the *meaning* of history, etc. We can also say that these are the ethical and religious problems, but placed on that particular foundation on which anything must be placed if it is to make sense to us.

In this way the idea of a universal philosophy is realized. Yet it is a realization altogether different from the one envisaged by Descartes and his age, influenced as they were by the natural sciences. Universal philosophy is not a universal system based on a theory of deduction — as if reality were a matter of calculation — but it is *a system of phenomenologically correlated disciplines* at the root of which we do not find the axiom *ego cogito*, but all-embracing self-examination.

In other words, the necessary path to knowledge which can be ultimately justified in the highest sense — or, what is the same, knowledge that is philosophical — is the path of *universal self-knowledge*, first in a monadic and then in an intermonadic sense. The Delphic expression γνῶθι σεαυτόν has acquired new meaning. Positive science is science lost in the world. One must first lose the world through *epoché* so as to regain it in universal self-examination. *Noli foras ire,* said St. Augustine, *in te redi, in interiore homine habitat veritas.*[1]

---

[1] "Do not wish to go out; go back into yourself. Truth dwells in the inner man." *De vera religione* 39, n. 72. (Taken from D. Cairns' translation in the *Cartesian Meditations*, Martinus Nijhoff (1960), p. 157).